Complete Course in English Book 3

A NEW REVISED EDITION

Robert J. Dixson

**In collaboration with
J. Andújar**

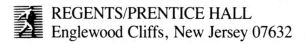
REGENTS/PRENTICE HALL
Englewood Cliffs, New Jersey 07632

Photo editor: Robert Sietsema
Cover design: Paul Gamarello
Text design: Judy Allan, The Designing Woman Concepts

 Published by Prentice-Hall, Inc.
A Simon & Schuster Company
Englewood Cliffs, New Jersey 07632

Printed in the United States of America

10 9 8 7 6 5

ISBN 0-13-158833-8

Prentice-Hall International (UK) Limited, *London*
Prentice-Hall of Australia Pty. Limited, *Sydney*
Prentice-Hall Canada Inc., *Toronto*
Prentice-Hall Hispanoamericana, S.A., *Mexico*
Prentice-Hall of India Private Limited, *New Delhi*
Prentice-Hall of Japan, Inc., *Tokyo*
Simon & Schuster Asia Pte. Ltd., *Singapore*
Editora Prentice-Hall do Brasil, Ltda., *Rio de Janeiro*

foreword

The revised editions of the four books of *Complete Course in English* make up a practical course stressing the conversational forms and everyday vocabulary of spoken American English. Each unit includes ample oral practice and encourages students to take an active role in their learning.

The texts are designed to be adaptable to a wide variety of teaching techniques. We suggest, however, that the teacher start each period with a review of the previous session's work before beginning a new lesson. Because the text introduces new grammar and new speech patterns at a steady rate, no more than one lesson should be covered in any session. The class should maintain a schedule of constant review and repetition and should not proceed to a new lesson until students have first demonstrated oral mastery of the current lesson.

Teachers should encourage students to learn full-form (complete sentence) patterns but also to learn and practice the more common, contracted-form patterns for use in their conversational English.

In Book 3, Units 11 and 20 are reviews of the vocabulary and grammar covered up to those points. Each of the other eighteen units has four parts: a dialogue, a grammar and usage section, an excercises section, and a reading and conversation section. The dialogue represents either a typical conversation which could take place between native speakers of American English or a short story which usually includes a brief conversation within it. This section also presents the points of grammar and usage introduced in the unit in a natural, conversational way. Following this section, there are ten questions about the dialogue or story. These questions will help the teacher test for comprehension and stimulate some conversation about the subject of the dialogue or story.

The grammar and usage and the exercises sections provide practice with important principles of grammar. A brief explanation is first given of the grammatical point in question; then some examples are provided. There follows next a series of simple exercises covering the point. Teachers may supplement these exercises by offering additional oral drills wherever possible. Oral drills and practice are important if a student is to be able to carry over the knowledge of the point and incorporate it into his or her everyday speech.

The reading and conversation sections contain a reading selection followed by a series of questions about the selection. Included also are questions designed to stimulate conversation and to expand on the subject of the reading. Following the questions are lists of the new words which have been introduced in the unit along with some special phrases for further vocabulary study. Teachers should use ingenuity to expand on the questions in the text and in the study of the vocabulary words and phrases, directing the students into conversational channels.

The final part of these sections is concerned with the pronunciation of all the important sounds of English. Teachers should have their students repeat the sounds both chorally and individually while guiding them and correcting errors in pronunciation.

contents

unit one

Dialogue

SUSAN: Hi, Eddie, this is Susan.

EDDIE: Hi, Susan. Where are you calling from?

SUSAN: I'm still here in Brazil, but I'll be coming to visit you next week on Thursday.

EDDIE: That's wonderful! When will your plane be arriving?

SUSAN: The woman at the airline office says we'll be landing at three o'clock in the afternoon. I hope you will have finished your classes by then.

EDDIE: Let me look at my schedule. *(He checks his class schedule.)* Yes, I will have taken my last class by noon on that day.

SUSAN: It's been so long since I've seen you. Do you know how long it has been?

EDDIE: By the time you arrive next week, it will have been about three or four months.

SUSAN: That's right. You left here on the tenth. By the time I arrive, you'll have been gone exactly four months.

EDDIE: Be sure you dress warmly. It may be hot in Brazil, but when you arrive here, it will probably be snowing. Will you be traveling alone on this trip, or will Tony be with you?

SUSAN: No, he won't be with me. I'll be flying alone this time. I hope this is a good time to visit. Will you be studying a lot while I'm there?

EDDIE: This is a perfect time for you to visit. By Thursday, I'll have finished my last midterm exam. I'll be free to show you all the sights in the city. At this time next week, you and I will be touring all the famous museums and historical sights.

SUSAN: Good, I am looking forward to it. Good-bye. I'll see you in a week.

Answer these questions:
  1. Why did Susan call Eddie?

2. Where was she calling from? Do you know where he is?
3. What will she be doing next week? When?
4. What does Susan ask about Eddie's classes on Thursday? How does he respond?
5. When Susan arrives, how long will it have been since she has seen Eddie?
6. What does Eddie think the weather will be when Susan arrives?
7. Will it be raining tomorrow morning when you wake up?
8. Will Susan be traveling with anyone?
9. What will Eddie have done by the time Susan arrives?
10. What does he think they'll be doing at this time next week?

Grammar and Usage

1. The Future Continuous Tense

a. Just as the past continuous tense describes an action which was going on or continuing at some definite point in the past, the future continuous tense describes an action which will be going on or continuing at some point in the future.

I *will be studying* when you come.

(Compare with the past continuous form: I *was studying* when you came.)

They *will be eating* when we get there.

b. The future continuous tense is formed in the same way as the continuous form of all other tenses. The verb *to be* is used as an auxiliary, and to this auxiliary is added the present participle of the main verb. See the Appendix for the full conjugation of the continuous form.

2. The Future Perfect Tense

The future perfect tense is formed with the future tense of the verb *to have,* used as an auxiliary, and the past participle of the main verb. The future perfect tense is used to describe an action which, at some point of time in the future, will be a past or completed action.

> By December, all the leaves *will have fallen* from the trees.
>
> On January 10, I *will have been* here six months.

Exercises

A. Supply the future continuous tense of the verb in parentheses.
1. When you get home tonight, I will be sleeping. (sleep)
2. If you come at noon, we _____ lunch. (eat)
3. At six o'clock tomorrow morning, they _____ . (get up)
4. She probably _____ in her garden at that hour. (work)
5. At this time next year, you _____ at a university in Brazil. (study)
6. Don't come at ten o'clock; Bill _____ his piano lesson then. (have)
7. Tomorrow afternoon at this time, we _____ over the Caribbean. (fly)
8. By the time you get here, it _____ . (rain)

B. Change the following from the past continuous to the future continuous tense.
1. He was sleeping by eleven o'clock. (He'll be sleeping when I arrive.)
2. She was working in her garden at the time.
3. They were having their dinner at seven o'clock.
4. The sun was shining at that hour.
5. We were watching TV at the time of the shooting.
6. They were getting ready to go to the ballet at six-thirty.
7. Were you eating dinner then?
8. Was he listening to the stereo or watching TV?

C. Underline the correct form.
1. When I got there, he (will be eating/was eating).
2. When you get there, he (will be eating/was eating).
3. I think he (eats/is eating) now.

4. (Were you/Will you be) finished by tomorrow afternoon?
5. By the end of next week, how long (will you have been/will you be) in Brazil?
6. By then, I (will have lived/will be living) there for six months.
7. I ('ll be waiting/waited) for you on the same corner tomorrow morning.
8. She says that she is sure they (will have completed/completed) the new road by June.

D. Supply the future perfect tense of the verbs in parentheses.
   1. By next Sunday, Eddie <u>will have been</u> in New York for six months. (be)
   2. When you arrive, all the others _____ . (leave)
   3. By the time we get there, the show _____ . (end)
   4. By November, all the leaves _____ from the trees. (fall)
   5. By next September, she _____ here thirty years. (work)
   6. By this time next month, all the flowers _____ . (die)
   7. We _____ in this country for two years on January 14. (be)
   8. _____ you _____ the book by tonight? (read)

E. Change the first verb in these sentences from past perfect to future perfect. Change the other verb from the past to the present.
   1. They had left when we arrived. (They will have left when we arrive.)
   2. The party had begun when we got there.
   3. The leaves had fallen from the trees by the time we went on vacation.
   4. He had finished the work when we saw him.
   5. She had come and gone when I arrived.
   6. You had already written the letter when you heard the news.
   7. She had spent all the money by the end of the year.
   8. We had forgotten all about it when the school year ended.

Reading and Conversation: The Arab in the Desert

An Arab was walking alone through the desert when he met two men.

"Have you lost one of your camels?" he asked them.

"Yes," they said.

"Was he blind in the right eye and lame in the left foot?" asked the Arab.

"Yes, he was."

"Had he lost a tooth, and was he carrying a cargo of honey and of corn?"

"Yes," said the men. "Please tell us where he is."

"I don't know where he is," said the Arab. "I have never seen such an animal nor have I talked with anyone about him."

The two men looked at each other in surprise. They were sure the Arab was deceiving them. Finally, they came up close to him, took hold of him, and demanded, "Where is the camel? And what have you done with the jewels which were hidden in the cargo?"

The Arab insisted that he had never seen the camel. The men finally forced him to go with them to a nearby town, where they took him before a police officer. They claimed that the Arab had stolen their camel.

"I have never seen their camel," insisted the Arab. "I am a simple man of the desert, and I have learned to look carefully at everything I see and to consider its importance. This morning, I saw the tracks of a camel which was lost. I knew it was lost because there were no human tracks near the tracks of the camel. I also saw that the camel must be blind in the right eye because the grass on that side of the tracks was left untouched, while the grass on the other side was eaten. The animal was lame because with one foot he left a track much lighter than any of the others. I knew he had lost a tooth because wherever he ate grass there was always a small space left untouched. I also found near the tracks of the camel groups of ants which were pulling pieces of corn. I also found groups of flies which were eating drops of honey along the way. From these facts, I was able to tell what cargo the animal was carrying."

6

A. Comprehension and Conversation

1. What is a *desert?* Name some of the famous deserts in the world.
2. Whom did the Arab meet? What had they lost?
3. What does *blind* mean? What is the meaning of *lame?*
4. What was wrong with the camel's mouth?
5. What did the two men think when the Arab told them he had never seen their camel? Would you have believed him?
6. How did the Arab know that the camel was lost? How did he know that it was blind in one eye?
7. How did he know that the camel was lame in one foot? How did he know the cargo the camel was carrying?
8. Why are camels used so frequently for carrying cargo in the desert?
9. Do you think the camel in the story was young or old? Why?
10. Did the Arab in the story turn out to be a thief?

B. Vocabulary

Nouns		Verbs	Adjectives
ant	honey	check	blind
Arab	human	claim	Caribbean
ballet	jewel	complete	historical
camel	museums	consider	lame
cargo	noon	deceive	untouched
corn	schedule	demand	
desert	sights	force	
flies	stereo	insist	Adverb
flower	track	land	frequently
garden		look forward to	
grass		tour	

C. Expressions

Use each of these expressions in a sentence.
That's wonderful!, it's been so long since . . . , that's right, by the time . . . , be sure, show (someone) the sights, good-bye.

D. Pronunciation Drill

θ   as in <u>th</u>in, au<u>th</u>or, heal<u>th</u>

thank	Thursday	both	mathematician
thing	thirty	method	south
think	three	birthday	north
through	thought	cloth	thirtieth

Mad River Canoe/Jim Henry

unit two

Dialogue

JACK: Hurry, Diane. You want to be there on time, don't you?

DIANE: Yes, I do. But I don't want to trip and fall.

JACK: I'm sorry. I'm just excited about being in the sailboat race.

DIANE: This is your first race, isn't it?

JACK: Yes, it is. I've sailed for many years, but this is my first race. You've sailed in races before, haven't you?

DIANE: Only twice before. I lost both times. I hope I don't lose again, but I don't think we have a chance of winning. I haven't practiced sailing in many months. You practice every day, don't you?

JACK: Yes, I do. The other day, my friend Bob said to me, "Jack, the way you're practicing, you can't lose, can you?" I said, "You're joking." He said he wasn't joking.

DIANE: Well, if Bob thinks we'll win, perhaps we'll win.

JACK: I don't know. The other contestants are pretty good sailors.

DIANE: Maybe we have a chance of winning after all. Now, let's hurry or we'll be late.

Answer these questions:

1. What does Diane mean when she says "trip and fall"?
2. Why does Jack want her to hurry? Where are they going?
3. What is a *sailboat?* How do people race sailboats?
4. Have you ever been in a sailboat race? Have you ever sailed?
5. What happened in Diane's other two races?
6. What did Jack's friend Bob say to him about the race?
7. What other kinds of boats, besides sailboats, can you name?
8. What kinds of races do you usually enjoy?
9. Does Diane think they're going to win the race?

10. What does *joking* mean? Give an example of something you have said when you were joking.

Grammar and Usage

Tag Endings

There is no exact equivalent in other languages for the tag ending in English. This construction is added to the end of a sentence to express a weak form of question. It is also used to invite confirmation of some fact we already know. A tag ending contains a pronoun and an auxiliary verb based on the original sentence; it contains no main verb. We use negative tag endings after affirmative sentences and affirmative tag endings after negative sentences.

> She is a Texan, <u>isn't she?</u>
> He speaks English well, <u>doesn't he?</u>
> They aren't in your class, <u>are they?</u>
> You can't finish it, <u>can you?</u>
> Mary will do it, <u>won't she?</u>
> It hasn't rained today, <u>has it?</u>

Exercises

A. Supply the appropriate tag ending.
1. You live in that building. (You live in that building, don't you?)
2. The sun is shining today.
3. It will be a new experience.
4. Those people are very polite.
5. The sun sets at six o'clock.
6. The traffic was very heavy.
7. They went into the museum.
8. You can speak Chinese.
9. They don't like to shop in that shopping center.
10. I don't need my umbrella today.
11. She won't be here today.

    12. He couldn't find a seat on the bus.
    13. You can't speak Farsi.
    14. It isn't snowing today.
    15. The lesson hasn't ended yet.
    16. John doesn't have to study tonight.

B. Underline the correct form.
    1. He said that he (will/would) be back soon.
    2. Do you know (if/which) she speaks English?
    3. I (said/told) them they could go.
    4. Do you mind (helping/to help) me?
    5. If I (had known/knew) your telephone number, I would have called you.
    6. He wants (me to come/that I come) back later.
    7. Listen! It (starts/is starting) to rain.
    8. If I (were/was) you, I'd tell him about it.

C. Change these sentences first to the past tense, then to the future tense, adding the appropriate tag endings.
    1. She speaks Turkish well, doesn't she? (She spoke Turkish well, didn't she? She'll speak Turkish well, won't she?)
    2. It doesn't snow in the spring, does it?
    3. You're busy, aren't you?
    4. Tony is out of town, isn't he?
    5. She can't swim, can she?
    6. You have piano lessons twice a week, don't you?
    7. The sun is hot, isn't it?
    8. They watch TV every night, don't they?

Reading and Conversation: Politeness

In many countries, the quality of politeness is considered extremely important. Japan is such a country. Compared to North Americans, the Japanese as a people are very polite. But sometimes it is difficult to be polite in a foreign language.

A Japanese student was in the United States studying at an American university. He did not know English well and wanted very much to learn the various expressions of politeness used in everyday conversation. He had been invited to a party at the home of one of his professors. He bought a book with many expressions of politeness in it, and he studied the expressions carefully. That afternoon at the professor's home when the professor's wife served him coffee and sandwiches, he got up at once, smiled happily, and said: "Thank you, sir or madam, as the case may be."

Another story concerns a Japanese executive who was in the United States on business. The maid in the guest house where the man was staying was told to be particularly polite to the foreign guest. The executive had to get up early one morning and asked the maid to wake him up at six o'clock. At exactly six o'clock the next morning, the maid entered the room of the Japanese executive and left a message on the table alongside the sleeping man's bed. At eleven o'clock the Japanese executive woke up, looked at his watch, and jumped out of bed. The message on the table said, "Dear Sir, it is now exactly six o'clock. Please get up at once."

A. Comprehension and Conversation

1. What is *politeness?* Are you a polite person?
2. Where was the Japanese student studying?
3. Where had he been invited?
4. What book did he buy? Why?
5. Where was the Japanese executive staying?
6. When did he want to get up? Whom did he ask to wake him up?
7. What happened when he woke up the next morning?
8. Why is it sometimes difficult to be polite in a foreign language?
9. What is the difference between politeness in your native language and politeness in English? Give some examples of each.
10. When should a person use the expressions *thank you, excuse me, please,* and *I beg your pardon?*

B. Vocabulary

	Nouns	*Verbs*	*Adjectives*	*Adverbs*
chance	maid	hurry	everyday	extremely
contestants	quality	invite	excited	particularly
conversation	race	joke	foreign	
executive	sailboat	practice	important	*Other*
experience	traffic	sail	Japanese	alongside
expression		trip	polite	both
		wake		
		(someone)		
		up		

C. Expressions

Use each of these expressions in a sentence.

on time, have a chance, the traffic was heavy, compared to, on business, I beg your pardon.

D. Pronunciation Drill

æ   as in can, man, and ask

can	fast	ask	class
have	black	hand	bad
man	and	hat	natural
apple	after	Saturday	last

Grumman

unit three

Dialogue

GLENN: Where are you going this afternoon?

AMY: I'm going to the courthouse. I'm supposed to meet Jim there in the lobby.

GLENN: Didn't Jim use to live in that neighborhood?

AMY: Yes, he did. That's why I'm going to meet him. He's going to show me the sights in that part of town. I'm supposed to be there at three o'clock.

GLENN: I used to go to school in that part of town. I would get off the bus at the courthouse and walk three blocks to my school. Then, of course, I'd walk to the opposite corner and take the same bus home.

AMY: My parents used to work over there, too. I'm the only one who has never been there, it seems.

GLENN: I think you'll like it. It's hard to get there, however. There's only one bus every hour, so be sure you don't miss your bus. It's supposed to leave here at two-fifteen, but sometimes it leaves early. I used to take the bus every day, so I know what I'm talking about.

AMY: Thanks for the advice. I used to have that problem with the bus I took to school. I'd get to the bus stop on time, but then I'd discover that the bus had left a few minutes early.

GLENN: Well, if your bus is supposed to leave at two-fifteen, perhaps you should leave now.

Answer these questions:
1. Where is Amy going this afternoon?
2. Whom is she supposed to meet? When is she supposed to meet him?
3. What is Jim going to show her?
4. Where did Jim use to live?
5. Where did Glenn use to go to school?
6. Where did you use to live?
7. What are you supposed to do this afternoon?

8. When is Amy's bus supposed to leave? Why should she leave now?
9. What used to happen when Amy took the school bus?
10. When are we supposed to finish this lesson? This book?

Grammar and Usage

1. *Supposed to*

a. *Supposed to* shows obligation to fulfill some promise or expectation.

   He *is supposed to* come back here at two o'clock.
   They *are supposed to* send the material tomorrow.

b. Note that the phrase is passive in form and the obligation is implied because the subject is expected or supposed by someone else to perform some action.

   He *is supposed* (by us) *to* leave today.
   The boat *is supposed* (by everyone) *to* arrive this afternoon.

2. *Used to*

a. The phrase *used to* is used to describe an action which continued habitually or for some period of time in the past but which does not take place now.

   He *used to* smoke. (He smoked for some time in the past, but he does not smoke now.)
   I *used to* buy my clothes in thrift shops. (Now I buy them in other stores.)

b. When it is awkward to repeat the phrase *used to* in a series, we often use *would* to give the same meaning of a continued or habitual action in the past.

   We *used to* go fishing together. We *would* get up every morning at six. Then we *would* have our breakfast.

Exercises

A. Supply the correct form of *supposed to*.
1. Helen <u>is supposed to meet</u> us at five o'clock this afternoon. (meet)
2. They _____ me the book last week. (send)
3. I _____ a composition tonight. (write)
4. It _____ yesterday, but it didn't. (rain)
5. _____ we _____ to our seats now? (go)
6. _____ she _____ here last night? (be)
7. We _____ not _____ before six o'clock tonight. (arrive)
8. They _____ not _____ the gifts before I arrived. (open)

B. Rewrite these sentences introducing the term *supposed to*.
1. We expect him to leave tomorrow. (He's supposed to leave tomorrow.)
2. They expect the plane to arrive at noon.
3. I don't expect her to bring the flowers with her.
4. They expected it to be delivered yesterday.
5. Do you expect the lesson to begin at ten o'clock?
6. Did you expect it to last an hour?
7. I didn't expect her to come by plane.
8. Didn't you expect it to be a beautiful day?

C. Change these sentences from affirmative to negative.
1. He is supposed to call her at noon. (He isn't supposed to call her at noon.)
2. The sailboat race was supposed to begin at one o'clock.
3. We were supposed to meet them on Riverside Drive.
4. It is supposed to be the longest suspension bridge in the world.
5. She was supposed to call me last night.
6. You were supposed to buy the tickets yesterday.
7. You are supposed to return the library books next week.
8. I'm supposed to finish this soon.

D. Repeat Exercise C, first changing the statements to simple
   questions, then changing them to questions with such words
   as *when, where, what time, why,* etc.
   1. He is supposed to call her at noon. (Is he supposed to call
      her at noon? When is he supposed to call her?)

E. Rewrite these sentences, introducing *used to* and adding
   some further information.
   1. She smoked a lot. (She used to smoke a lot, but now she
      doesn't.)
   2. I caught a lot of pigeons.
   3. I played the piano well.
   4. She was a very good swimmer.
   5. He rode the bus to school.
   6. You were able to speak Spanish.

Reading and Conversation: Catching Pigeons

Although we are always taught that we should work hard and
try to improve our situation in life, we must also learn, at times,
to be satisfied with what we have. A former president of the
United States once told the following story about himself:

"When I was a boy, I used to spend a lot of time trying to
catch the pigeons which would fly into our backyard from time
to time. I used a large wooden box about three feet long and
three feet wide. I would raise one end of the box several feet in
the air by placing under it a piece of wood to which I had tied a
long cord. I used to place pieces of corn under the box; then I
would hide at a distance, perhaps behind a tree, until the
pigeons came to eat the corn. When the pigeons were under the
box, I would pull the cord, the end of the box would fall, and the
pigeons would be caught.

"One day, a large number of pigeons flew into the yard. There
were ten of them in all. Nine of the pigeons flew immediately to
the corn under the box, but the tenth pigeon remained outside. I
could not decide whether to pull the cord and catch the nine
pigeons or wait until the tenth pigeon also came to eat the corn.
I waited, but soon one of the nine pigeons left the box. Perhaps
this ninth pigeon and also the tenth pigeon would return? I

waited. Then another pigeon left the box. What should I do? Then the seventh pigeon left. I could not be satisfied now with only six pigeons, when I could have caught nine before. Soon the sixth pigeon left, and, one by one, the others followed, until there was not a single pigeon under the box. Finally, they all flew away. I was disappointed, and I was also angry with myself for being so stupid. But I had learned that it is sometimes better to be satisfied with what you have than to try to catch *all ten pigeons.*"

A. Comprehension and Conversation

1. What is a *pigeon?* Are there many pigeons in your neighborhood? What kinds of birds can you see in your neighborhood?
2. What did the former president use to catch pigeons with when he was young?
3. Why did he place the corn under the box?
4. What would happen when he pulled the cord?
5. How many pigeons flew into the yard in the story he told? How many flew under the box?
6. Why did he wait? Why didn't he pull the cord and catch the nine pigeons?
7. What was the result of his waiting?
8. What lesson did he learn from the experience?
9. Have you ever tried to catch birds? Have you caught any other animals? How?
10. What is the moral of this story?

B. Vocabulary

Nouns		*Verbs*	*Other*
advice	gift	be satisfied	although
block	lobby	last	
bridge	neighborhood		
bus stop	piece	*Adjectives*	
composition	pigeon	disappointed	
cord	situation	following	
courthouse		former	
		wooden	

C. Expressions

Use each of these expressions in a sentence.
of course, catch a bus, over there, it seems, spend a lot of
time, from time to time, in all, a large number of.

D. Pronunciation Drill

I as in _it_, b_ui_ld, b_ee_n

it	his	sick	big	wish
if	sit	which	bring	winter
in	think	little	miss	with
is	wind	thing	pigeon	important

unit four

Dialogue

LUCY: Pablo, how long have you been living in Washington, D.C.?

PABLO: I've been studying at George Washington University for three years, but I came here a year before that in order to study English. I've been living here for four years.

LUCY: Were you here when they opened the new subway system?

PABLO: Yes, I had been living here for about a month when the Metro opened. Actually, the subway had been operating for several years but not in my neighborhood, so I never rode it. Thanks for meeting me here at the university. Have you been waiting long?

LUCY: No, only about ten minutes. I've been watching all the other students. They seem to come from all parts of the world.

PABLO: The school has been offering courses which appeal to students from many countries for many years. In fact, I've been living with two students who are from distant parts of the world. I'm from Peru, and my two roommates are from Korea and Nigeria.

LUCY: Have you known them for a long time?

PABLO: Almost four years. I had only been attending English classes for about a week when I met them. We've been rooming together since then. We get along well together. Here they are! Come, I want you to meet them.

LUCY: Good. I've been hoping you would introduce me.

Answer these questions:
1. How long has Pablo been living in Washington?
2. How long have you been living in your present home?
3. How long had he been living there when the Metro opened?

4. How long had you been studying English when you started this book?
5. How long had Lucy been waiting for Pablo when he arrived?
6. How long had you been waiting for your bus or train this morning when it arrived?
7. How long has Pablo been living with his two roommates?
8. How long has he been studying English?
9. How long have you been sitting in your chair today?
10. How long have you been studying English? (Give the year.)

Grammar and Usage

1. The Present Perfect Continuous Tense

The present perfect continuous tense is used to describe an action which began in the past and continues in the present.

He *has been studying* English for two years.
How long *has* he *been studying* English?
I *have been living* here since 1983.
Have you *been living* here since 1983?

2. The Past Perfect Continuous Tense

a. The past perfect continuous tense is used to describe some continuous action which continued up to some definite point in the past.

He *had been studying* for two hours when we arrived.
He *had been living* there two years when the war began.

b. The continuous form of both the present perfect tense and the past perfect tense is formed in the same way as the continuous form of all other tenses. We use the verb *to be* as an auxiliary and add to this auxiliary the present participle of the main verb. See the Appendix for the full conjugation of the continuous form.

Exercises

A. Supply the present perfect continuous tense of the verbs in parentheses.
   1. She <u>has been living</u> here for several years. (live)
   2. I _____ there since 1983. (work)
   3. Carl _____ at George Washington University for about three years. (study)
   4. He _____ English all his life. (speak)
   5. _____ you _____ for me for a long time? (wait)
   6. _____ it _____ all day? (rain)
   7. We _____ to reach you by phone for hours. (try)
   8. How long _____ you _____ on the phone? (talk)

B. Rewrite these sentences, changing the tense from the simple present perfect to the present perfect continuous.
   1. She's worked in this office since 1980. (She's been working in this office since 1980.)
   2. He's lived here for many years.
   3. How long have you lived here?
   4. I have ridden the Metro since it opened.
   5. You have sat on that bench for over two hours.
   6. Have you drunk coffee since you were a child?
   7. How long have you studied English?
   8. I've sailed boats for many years.

C. Supply the past perfect continuous tense of the verbs in parentheses.
   1. He <u>had been waiting</u> for several hours when we arrived. (wait)
   2. She _____ there for two years when the war began. (live)
   3. When I first met them, they _____ for six months. (work)
   4. How long _____ Bill _____ English when he first went to the United States? (study)
   5. I _____ French for years before I wrote the book. (teach)
   6. She _____ a long time when I woke her. (sleep)
   7. He _____ too hard, and that is why he got sick. (work)

8. I _____ it wrong, but then I learned how to do it correctly. (do)

D. Rewrite these sentences, changing the tense from the simple past perfect to the past perfect continuous.
   1. He had read the letter when we arrived. (He had been reading the letter when we arrived.)
   2. They had talked about it when I met them.
   3. She had had her music lesson when I called.
   4. He had eaten his dinner when we arrived.
   5. They had lost a lot of money in their business.
   6. Had you played the piano when the police arrived?
   7. Did you say you had studied English?
   8. He told me that he had worked there.

Reading and Conversation: An Experiment with Tea and Coffee

Most of the foods which we eat today were, at one time or another, unknown to us. One by one, they were introduced and became a part of our everyday diet. Did you ever wonder about the courage of the first people to try these foods? Who, for example, ate the first oyster? Who had the courage to eat the first mushroom?

When tea and coffee were introduced into Europe in the eighteenth century, there were many arguments for and against their use. Some people claimed that coffee and tea were poison and that, if drunk over long periods of time, they would kill a person. In Sweden, King Gustav III decided to find out whether these claims were true or false. It happened that there were two brothers who were in prison at the time; they were twins and were almost exactly alike in every way. They had also been condemned to die. The king decided to let them live if one of the men agreed to drink several cups of tea each day and the other, several cups of coffee each day.

Both brothers lived many years without any problems of any kind. At last, the brother who had to drink tea every day died at the age of eighty-three; the other died a few years later.

Because of the way the experiment had turned out, Sweden is

today one of the countries of the world where much tea and coffee are drunk.

A. Comprehension and Conversation

1. What different foods have you eaten in the past twenty-four hours?
2. Which of these foods were eaten by people five hundred years ago? One hundred years ago?
3. Have you ever eaten oysters? Mushrooms? Do you like them?
4. What did people in Europe believe about coffee and tea in the eighteenth century?
5. Which is more popular in your country, coffee or tea? Which do you think is more popular in the United States?
6. Who was Gustav III? What did he decide to do?
7. What was the twins' sentence? How old were they when they died?
8. What did the king's experiment prove?
9. Do you drink coffee? Tea? Do you like these beverages?
10. Name some foods which you have not tried. Would you like to try them someday?

B. Vocabulary

Nouns		Verbs	Adjectives
bench	poison	agree	distant
beverage	prison	appeal	unknown
century	roommate	condemn	
courage	subway	find out	Other
course	system	offer	ago
diet	twin	operate	
experiment	war	try (food)	
mushroom		turn out	
oyster		wonder about	

C. Expressions

Use each of these expressions in a sentence.

in order to, in fact, at one time or another, one by one, for example, for and against, true or false, at last.

D. Pronunciation Drill

i   as in m<u>e</u>, b<u>ea</u>t, chi<u>ef</u>ly

eat	be	feel	read
easy	see	we	speak
each	three	she	seen
teacher	me	movie	weak
only	maybe	thieves	people

unit five

Dialogue

JOYCE: Thanks for inviting me to Central Park, Bob. I haven't been feeling well lately, and I think this picnic will help me feel better.

BOB: I'm glad you could come. You'd better keep your coat on, though. It might get chilly later.

JOYCE: I will. You know, the most surprising thing about Central Park, Bob, is its size.

BOB: You're right. I read that this park is two and a half miles long and a half mile wide. And, of course, it's in the middle of New York City. The land on which the park lies is worth a great deal of money.

JOYCE: In other words, the city hasn't been selling any of the land for use as office buildings or apartments. Is that right?

BOB: Right. When New York City bought the land in 1856, it was mostly farmland. A great deal of the land was on the outskirts of the city.

JOYCE: You were right about the weather, Bob. It is getting chilly. I think I'd better keep this coat on.

BOB: If you'd rather go inside, we can always eat in one of the pavilions at the zoo.

JOYCE: I would rather stay here, but you're probably right. I should go indoors. I don't want this cold to get any worse.

BOB: Smart thinking. Let's go.

Answer these questions:
1. Where is this conversation taking place? In what city?
2. How has Joyce been feeling lately? How have you been feeling lately?
3. Why does Bob tell Joyce she had better keep her coat on?
4. How big is Central Park?
5. What does Bob say about the value of the land in Central Park?

6. When did New York buy the land for Central Park? What was the land used for then?
7. Why does Joyce think she'd better keep her coat on?
8. What does Bob suggest?
9. What does Joyce say she'd rather do?
10. What is a *pavilion*? A *zoo*? A *picnic*?

Grammar and Usage

1. *Had better/would rather*

a. Two important idiomatic phrases are *had better* and *would rather*. Both are followed by the infinitive form of the main verb without *to*. Both refer to present or future time; both are generally used in contracted form.

"You *had better* (You'*d better*) *spend* more time on your homework" means that it will be better or it is advisable for you to spend more time on your homework. Other examples follow:

He *had better* (He'*d better*) *see* a doctor at once about those headaches he has been having.

You *had better* (You'*d better*) not *say* anything to her about it.

"I *would rather* (I'*d rather*) *wait* outside" means the same as "I prefer to wait outside." Other examples follow:

I *would rather* (I'*d rather*) *walk* than go by taxi.

He said he *would rather* (he'*d rather*) not *discuss* it with her.

b. Note the formation of the negative and question forms of these phrases.

You'*d better* *not* say anything about it.

Hadn't you *better* tell her about it?

I'*d rather* *not* discuss it.

Wouldn't you *rather* go indoors?

2. The Negative Form with Two Auxiliaries

To form the negative in sentences where there are two

auxiliary verbs, place *not* after the first auxiliary.

He has been studying for two hours.

He has *not* been studying for two hours.

She should have told him about it.

She shouldn*'t* have told him about it.

3. *A great deal of*

The phrase *a great deal of* is used with singular nouns as a synonym for *much* or *a lot of*. It cannot be used with plural nouns.

He has a lot of money.

He has *a great deal of* money.

Has there been much snow in Maine this year?

Has there been *a great deal of* snow in Maine this year?

Exercises

A. Rewrite these sentences, introducing the phrase *had better*. Use contractions where possible.
   1. You should wait for me outside. (You'd better wait for me outside.)
   2. I should come back a little later.
   3. You should go to the hospital at once.
   4. You shouldn't mention it to him today.
   5. Shouldn't you wear a coat in this weather?
   6. It would be a good idea for you to take some food with you.
   7. It would be a good idea for you to wear a heavier coat.
   8. It would not be a good idea for you to see that movie.

B. Answer these questions using the contracted form of *would rather*.
   1. Would you rather sit in the first row or the second? (I'd rather sit in the second row.)
   2. Would you rather have your class in the morning or afternoon?
   3. Did he say that he'd rather travel by plane or by train?
   4. In which of those two restaurants would you rather eat?

    5. If you could visit Asia, would you rather visit Japan or China?
    6. Would she rather go to a movie tonight or watch TV?
    7. Would they rather visit us or stay home tonight?
    8. Would you rather watch a drama or a comedy?

C. Change these sentences to the negative form.
    1. He's been working here for five years. (He hasn't been working here for five years.)
    2. She'd been sleeping when we saw her.
    3. I will have been here for two weeks next Monday.
    4. They should be roller-skating in the park.
    5. They will be having dinner at seven o'clock tonight.
    6. By tomorrow, he will have forgotten all about it.
    7. They have been looking at the animals in the zoo.
    8. I had been talking in my sleep.

D. Substitute *a great deal of* for *much* or *a lot of* in the following sentences.
    1. Do you spend much time on your English? (Do you spend a great deal of time on your English?)
    2. Do you have much work to do today?
    3. He drinks a lot of coffee.
    4. She makes a lot of money.
    5. There has been a lot of rain lately.
    6. There hasn't been much snow lately.
    7. My pen doesn't seem to use much ink.
    8. Do you do a lot of business with them?

Reading and Conversation: An Incident at the Post Office

My friend Hal works at the post office. Hal is usually a calm, friendly fellow, but the other day he acted very strangely when Mr. Boswell came in to buy some stamps.

Mr. Boswell asked Hal for ten 25-cent stamps. Hal looked at him and said, "Why don't you buy ten 15-cent stamps and ten 10-cent stamps? That way you'll get more stamps for the same money."

Mr. Boswell looked at Hal as though he were crazy. "Why should I bother with all that when ten 25-cent stamps are all I need? Don't you have any 25-cent stamps?"

"Certainly we do. What kind of post office do you think this is?"

"Well, then, give me the 25-cent stamps and let me get out of here."

"Have you tried our new airmail stamps?" Hal then asked pleasantly. "They don't cost much more and they're very pretty. We also have a special commemorative series honoring famous American athletes. They're very attractive."

By now, Mr. Boswell was getting upset. "Listen," he said, "keep your stamps, all of them. I can buy my stamps somewhere else." He then turned around and angrily walked out of the post office, slamming the door behind him.

Hal turned to me and explained. "He's the owner of an office supply store. Every time I go in there, he drives me crazy trying to sell me everything he has in the shop. Now I think we're even."

A. Comprehension and Conversation

1. Where does this incident take place? Do all of the people in the story know each other?
2. Why is Mr. Boswell in the post office?
3. Who is Hal? What does he try to sell Mr. Boswell?
4. How much does it cost to send a letter in your country? How much does it cost to send one to the United States?
5. Why did Mr. Boswell get upset and walk out angrily?
6. What does *to slam* a door mean? Have you ever slammed a door? Why?
7. What is an *office supply store?* What can you buy in one?
8. How did Hal get even with Mr. Boswell?
9. Why do people want to *get even* with other people? Have you ever wanted to get even with someone? When? Why?
10. Where is the nearest post office? What can you do in a post office?

B. Vocabulary

Nouns		Verbs	Adjectives	Adverb
Asia	owner	be roller-skating	attractive	inside
cold (virus)	pavilion	be worth	calm	
drama	picnic	bother with	chilly	
farmland	shop	feel good	half	*Other*
incident	value	get upset		even
mile		lie		indoors
outskirts		slam		though

C. Expressions

Use each of these expressions in a sentence.
in other words, a good idea, a little later, as though, (to) drive someone crazy, somewhere else.

D. Pronunciation Drill

Z   as in zoo, easy, lose

is	days	lazy	design
does	knows	busy	years
has	rains	comes	was
chairs	grows	as	nose

unit six

Dialogue

CAROL: How are you feeling, David? You look sad.

DAVID: I'm feeling homesick. I wish I were back home in Argentina. I miss my family, my friends, my neighborhood, my horse, and my music.

CAROL: Your music?

DAVID: Yes, the kind of music people listen to in my hometown is different from the music people listen to in New York.

CAROL: I know what you mean. I often wish I had some tapes or records of the music of my country.

DAVID: I wish I knew some other Argentinians. Perhaps that would help me overcome my homesickness.

CAROL: I have an idea! Let's go to that new Argentinian restaurant over on Second Avenue, Las Pampas. A friend of mine who went there told me it was very good.

DAVID: That sounds wonderful!

CAROL: He also said that when he heard the music there it was as though he were really in Argentina. I wish I had gone with him, but we can go tonight, if you'd like.

DAVID: I'd love it! It would be wonderful to feel as if I had returned to my home. I'd enjoy feeling as though we were sitting in a restaurant in Mendoza.

CAROL: Let's go now.

Answer these questions:
1. Why does David look sad? Have you ever been home-sick? Where were you?
2. Where does he wish he were? What does he miss?
3. What does he say about his music?
4. What kind of music do you enjoy? What kind of music do your parents enjoy?
5. Do you have any tapes or records? By whom?
6. Where is Buenos Aires? Where is Argentina?
7. What does "feeling as though we were sitting in a restaurant in Mendoza" mean?

8. What kinds of restaurants do you enjoy?
9. Did you ever go to another city and feel as though you had been there before? Describe the feeling.
10. Do you ever wish you were someone else? Who?

Grammar and Usage

1. The Subjunctive after *wish*

Since the verb *to wish* always suggests a situation which is unreal or contrary to fact, it is followed by the subjunctive mood. Just as with conditional statements, a past tense is used to show present time, and a past perfect tense is used to show past time.

> I wish I *knew* English well.
> I wish I *had gone* with you last night.
> He wishes he *were* in New York now.

2. The Subjunctive after *as if* and *as though*

Since the conjunctions *as if* and *as though* also indicate a situation which is unreal or contrary to fact, they are also followed by the subjunctive. A past tense is used to show present time, and a past perfect tense is used to show past time.

> He looks *as if* he *were* very sick.
> He looked *as though* he *had lost* his last friend.

Exercises

A. Supply the correct form of the verb in parentheses.
1. John wishes he <u>knew</u> how to swim. (know)
2. I wish I _____ to the movie with you last night. (go)
3. She wishes she _____ college. (finish)
4. I wish today _____ a holiday; I'd go to the beach. (be)
5. They wish that they _____ studying English several years ago. (start)
6. I wish I _____ about this yesterday. (know)
7. Did you ever wish you _____ someone else? (be)

8. I wish yesterday _____ a holiday; I'd have gone to the beach. (be)
9. He treated her as if she _____ the contest. (win)
10. She treats him as if he _____ an old friend. (be)
11. You look as though you _____ the whole night studying. (spend)
12. You talk as though you _____ in the United States for many years. (live)
13. He acted as though he _____ never _____ us. (see)
14. She laughed as though someone _____ a joke. (tell)
15. Don't you think she looks as though she _____ tired? (be)
16. Is Ken acting as if he _____ sick? (be)

B. Underline the correct form.
1. If I (was/were) you, I'd visit Barcelona.
2. I wish I (was/were) in your position.
3. If I (had/have) a car, I'd drive to the mountains.
4. I wish I (had/have) a car.
5. I wish I (could go/could have gone) with you to the concert last night.
6. He acts as if he (can/could) dance like Michael Jackson.
7. If yesterday (was/had been) a holiday, I'd have gone to the beach.
8. David often wishes he (has/had) some tapes and records of Argentinian music.

Reading and Conversation: The Three Wishes

Long ago, there lived a couple who had a dairy farm. They were poor and spent much of their time wishing for things they did not have.

Often the man would say, "I wish I were handsome" or "I wish I had more cows."

Frequently, the woman would say, "I wish I were wealthy" or "I wish I were a beautiful princess."

One day, some fairies heard their wishes and decided to conduct an experiment. They went to the couple and granted them three wishes. Whatever they wished would truly be granted.

The two of them talked a long time over what they should wish for. But after a while they became hungry, and from force of habit the woman suddenly said, "I wish I had some sausages to eat." Immediately her market basket was full of sausages.

Then a heated argument began because the husband said that his wife had wasted one of their valuable wishes on such a cheap thing as sausages. The argument grew hotter, and finally in anger the wife said, "I wish these sausages were hanging from your nose!" Of course, the sausages immediately flew to the poor man's nose and could not be removed.

Now, there was only one thing the poor woman could do. She really loved her husband, and so she had to spend their third wish in removing the sausages from his nose. Thus, except for a few sausages, they had nothing to show for their three wishes.

A. Comprehension and Conversation

1. What is a *dairy farm?* What kinds of animals live on such a farm?
2. Why did the couple spend much of their time wishing? How did they express their wishes?
3. What is a *fairy?* Do you think there are such things as fairies? What did the fairies decide?
4. What happened when the woman got hungry? If you had been hungry, what would you have wished for? Are you hungry now?
5. What happened when she wished for the food?
6. Why did the husband and wife begin arguing? What happened to the string of sausages?
7. How did they have to use their third wish? Why?
8. What is the moral of this story?
9. What does *force of habit* mean? Tell some things you do from force of habit.
10. Do you ever wish for things you do not possess? What things?

B. Vocabulary

Nouns		Verbs	Adjectives	Adverb
argument	music	conduct	handsome	truly
basket	nose	grant	heated	
couple	position	overcome	homesick	
cow	princess	spend time		
dairy	record	treat		
fairy	sausage	waste		
holiday	string			
horse	tape			
market				

C. Expressions

Use each of these expressions in a sentence.

I know what you mean, different from, at home, spend the night, in my hometown, conduct an experiment, after a while, nothing to show for.

D. Pronunciation Drill

V   as in very, have, of

very	leave	of	November
have	glove	several	every
live	above	native	never
five	over	favorite	visit

Jane Latta

unit seven

Dialogue

DAN: Hi, Sue. This is Dan.

SUE: Hi, Dan. It's good to hear your voice. Where are you?

DAN: I'm still here in Ottawa. I just called to discuss Mom and Dad's anniversary. What do you suggest we get them?

SUE: I recommend that we buy them a new stereo. I know they need one, because I've worn out the old one.

DAN: That's a good idea, but a stereo is a gift they'd have to share between them. I'd recommend that we get them each a present. I remember when I was a child, I didn't like to receive just one present that I had to share with you and our brothers.

SUE: I know what you mean. I wish Mom had demanded that Dad buy each of us a present. On the other hand, we have to remember that this is a celebration of an event that they shared—their wedding.

DAN: Well, I'll let you decide what to get. The stereo sounds good. Just let me know how much I owe you for my part. I assume we are all dividing the cost of the gift among us.

SUE: Yes, I figured that each of us would pay one-quarter of the cost.

DAN: I'm glad that's settled. Now, tell me how school is.

SUE: It's really hard this semester. My accounting teacher requires that we do a lot of homework every night.

DAN: Is this the teacher you told me about? The one we read about in the newspaper?

SUE: That's the one. He was also Bill's accounting teacher last year. He's pretty good. I guess I'm lucky to have him for this class.

DAN: Well, good luck.

Answer these questions:
1. Who called whom? Why?
2. What does Sue recommend they buy their parents as an anniversary present?

3. What does Dan suggest? Why?
4. What does Sue wish that her mother had done?
5. What do they decide to buy?
6. Who will pay for the gift? How will the cost be divided?
7. What does Sue's teacher require that she do?
8. What was the relationship between Sue's teacher and Bill last year?
9. What is *accounting?* Have you ever studied accounting?
10. Which school subject requires the most homework?

Grammar and Usage

1. The Subjunctive after Special Verbs

a. After such verbs as *suggest, demand, require,* and *recommend,* which indicate some possible or proposed situation, we use the subjunctive mood, present tense.

He recommended that she *wait.*
He insisted that I *be* there at noon.

b. The present tense, subjunctive mood of all verbs corresponds exactly to the indicative except in the third person singular, where the subjunctive form has no *s.* The verb *to be,* however, has a special subjunctive form.

to work

I	work	we	work
you	work	you	work
he she it	work	they	work

to be

I	be	we	be
you	be	you	be
he she it	be	they	be

2. *Between/among*

Between is generally used when referring to two persons or things. When referring to more than two persons or things, we use *among.*

He sat *between* Helen and Mary.
The four boys divided the money *among* themselves.

3. The Omission of *that, which,* and *whom*

a. Note that we often omit the word *that* when used as a conjunction introducing a noun clause. The omission of *that* in such cases does not change the meaning of the sentence in any way; *that* is understood but not expressed.

> He said *that* he would come.
> He said he would come.

b. Very often, especially in speaking, we also omit *that, whom,* and *which* when used as relative pronouns and when they are direct objects of the verb. Here again the omission does not change the meaning of the sentence; *that, whom,* and *which* are understood but not expressed.

> The man *that* I saw was Mr. Smith.
> The man I saw was Mr. Smith.
> Is this the teacher *whom* you told me about?
> Is this the teacher you told me about?
> The stereo is a gift *which* they'll have to share.
> The stereo is a gift they'll have to share.

Exercises

A. Supply the correct form of the verb in parentheses.
  1. He insisted that she <u>go</u> with them. (go)
  2. The teacher demands that everyone _____ in his or her seat by nine o'clock. (be)
  3. The doctor recommended that Peter _____ his medicine. (take)
  4. Sue suggested that she _____ a stereo for their parents. (buy)
  5. They demand that we _____ later. (come back)
  6. He requires that I _____ a lot of homework. (do)
  7. He recommends that each of us _____ a separate gift. (buy)
  8. Henry insists that we _____ in his office by noon. (be)

B. Rewrite these sentences, omitting the conjunction *that* and the relative pronouns *that, whom,* and *which.*
  1. He said that I should buy the book which he recom-

42

mended. (He said I should buy the book he recommended.)
2. She claimed that she was busy in school.
3. The girls whom I met at the party were not sisters.
4. Did you say that you had been sick a long time?
5. He pretended that he had come to sacrifice the prince.
6. The idea which you had was a good one.
7. The animals which we saw in the zoo were all asleep.
8. She didn't say that we were going to the museum.
9. I didn't say that the exhibits were interesting.
10. The stories which he told us were funny.
11. The shouts that we heard came from the boat.
12. Is this the one whom we read about in the newspaper?
13. The gift which she chose was not expensive.
14. The teacher that I saw was your teacher.
15. They said that their last name was Garcia.
16. I said that we were going to the opening of the museum.

C. Fill in the blanks with *between* or *among*.
1. She sat between her two sisters.
2. She sat _____ the twelve other students in the class.
3. Put her _____ Mary and me.
4. Was it difficult to find him _____ so many people?
5. The brother and sister divided the money _____ them.
6. The brothers and sisters divided the money _____ them.
7. There were four of them; they divided the pie _____ themselves.
8. I placed the card _____ the two books.

Reading and Conversation: A Clever Cure

A young prince had been sick for some time. In his feverish condition, he developed a strange idea. He thought he was a cow! Since it was the practice in his religion to sacrifice animals, he also insisted on being sacrificed like all the other cows. Finally, an old village doctor was called in to treat him. The old doctor pretended that he was a priest and that he had come to sacrifice the prince. He took out a long knife and began to feel the prince's arms and legs in order to find the best place to cut him. Then suddenly he stopped. He said that the cow was much too thin and weak to sacrifice. It would be an insult to their religion to sacrifice such a poor animal!

The prince was naturally very displeased. But he finally agreed with the doctor that he must get fatter if he wished to be sacrificed. He began to eat and drink great quantities of food. He ate and ate.

As the weeks passed, he grew fatter and fatter. But at the same time he also grew stronger, and his health improved. In fact, he soon felt so much better that he entirely forgot about being a cow!

A. Comprehension and Conversation

1. With whom is this story concerned? What was wrong with him?
2. Why did he insist that he be sacrificed?
3. What is the difference between an *old village doctor* and a *priest?*
4. Is it still the practice of some religions to sacrifice animals? Which religions?
5. What did the old doctor pretend to do?
6. What is an *insult?* Have you ever seen anyone insult another person?
7. Why was the prince displeased?
8. What happened when the prince began to eat and drink a lot?
9. Have you ever killed an animal? What kind?
10. What do you think of the old doctor's plan to trick the prince?

B. Vocabulary

Nouns

anniversary	leg	village
celebration	prince	voice
event	quarter	wedding
health	religion	

	Verbs		*Adjectives*
assume	figure	recommend	feverish
be called	improve	require	lucky
in	insist	sacrifice	
be settled	insult	share	*Adverb*
discuss	kill	suggest	just
divide	pretend	wear out	(only)

C. Expressions

Use these expressions in a sentence.
in other words, it sounds good, divided among us.

D. Pronunciation Drill

ə   as in c<u>u</u>p, l<u>o</u>ve, <u>a</u>go

us	love	trouble
up	come	enough
under	some	country
much	son	soda
cut	done	mama

unit eight

Dialogue

DENNIS: I'm glad I had my car washed yesterday. It looks new again.

FERNANDO: That reminds me, I should get my car washed, too. Which place do you take your car to?

DENNIS: I take it to John's City Service. I usually have my car serviced there, too. They're reasonable, and they're good workers.

FERNANDO: I need to get the oil changed in my car. Do you think I should take it to John's?

DENNIS: By all means. Whom did you take it to before?

FERNANDO: I took it to the dealer who sold me the car, but I wasn't satisfied with the work done.

DENNIS: Is that the place which you told me about last week—the place where they lost your keys?

FERNANDO: That's the place.

DENNIS: What did you take it there for?

FERNANDO: I didn't know they were such poor workers when I went there. Which of the mechanics at John's do you usually go to?

DENNIS: I usually go to John himself. He's an old friend. I get the car filled up with gas there, too. You ought to call him.

FERNANDO: Thanks. I will.

Answer these questions:
1. What did Dennis have done yesterday? Is he pleased?
2. What does Fernando want to do?
3. Why does Dennis have his car serviced at John's?
4. What is *oil?* Why does a car need to have its oil changed?
5. Where did Fernando take his car before now? Was he pleased?
6. What did he take it there for?

7. Where do you (or your parents) usually have your car filled with gas? Where do you have it serviced?
8. If your watch stops, where can you have it fixed?
9. If your TV breaks, where can you get it repaired?
10. Do you think Fernando will take his car to John's? Why?

Grammar and Usage

1. The Causative Form

When we wish to indicate an action which was performed by someone else (not ourselves) but was caused or instigated by us, we use either *to have* or *to get* and the past participle of the main verb.

> He often *has* his shoes *shined.* (by someone)
> She *had* her hair *cut.*
> I *got* the work *done* by an expert.
> *Did* she *get* her house *painted?*

2. The Position of Prepositions

a. Instead of placing a preposition directly before its object at the beginning of a sentence, we often place it, in conversational English, at the end of the sentence. This usage mainly involves prepositions used before *whom, which,* and *what.*

> Whom did you give it *to?*
> (*To* whom did you give it?)
> What do you want it *for?*
> Which window did you go *to?*

b. We also separate the preposition from its object and place it at the end of the clause in complex sentences where *whom, which,* or *what* form part of the subordinate or noun clause.

> He asked me *whom* you gave it *to.*
> He asked me *to whom* you gave it.
> This is the book *which* he told us *about.*
> This is the book *about which* he told us.
> I don't know *what* he wants it *for.*
> I don't know *for what* he wants it.

Exercises

A. Change each of these sentences to the causative form.
1. I cut my hair every month. (I get my hair cut every month.)
2. I must fix my watch.
3. He shines his shoes every day.
4. She washed her car yesterday.
5. We must paint our apartment.
6. Did he sign the letter?
7. Do they clean their suits there?
8. We didn't paint our house.

B. Place the italicized preposition at the end of the sentence or clause.
1. *To* whom did you give it? (Whom did you give it to?)
2. *For* what will she use it?
3. That is the teacher *with* whom we studied.
4. I asked him *for* what he needed the book.
5. *By* whom was it written?
6. *For* what did you ask me?
7. Is that the room *in* which you have your class?
8. Is she the person *for* whom you have been waiting?
9. I don't know *from* what country they come.
10. *About* what did you talk?
11. *At* what are you looking?
12. I couldn't understand *about* what you were talking.
13. You didn't tell me *with* whom you were traveling.
14. *From* what country do you come?

C. Underline the correct form.
1. He recommended that I (<u>be</u>/am) there by noon.
2. Pat sat (between/among) Sara and me.
3. Walter is the man with (who/whom) you spoke.
4. Terry (supposed to/is supposed to) be here by now.
5. He doesn't speak English well, (does he/doesn't he)?
6. I wish I (can/could) ski well.
7. The five players on the team could not agree (between/among) themselves.
8. He insisted that she (go/goes) with him.

Reading and Conversation: How to Have Your Hair Cut

My name is Tommy Jenkins, and I've been cutting hair in this town for over thirty years. The other day, I was having lunch with some of the other barbers in town. We started talking about some of the most interesting customers we had had. When it was my turn, I told them a story about something that happened to me about fifteen years ago. I've never forgotten it.

A man came into my barbershop holding the hand of a young boy. The man was in a great hurry, and he asked me to cut his hair first and then to do the boy's hair. The man sat in my chair, and the boy sat in the waiting area and read magazines.

Well, I cut the man's hair, and when I finished, he got out of the chair and seated the boy in it. He then excused himself and repeated that he was in a great hurry. He asked me to go ahead and cut the boy's hair. He said he would be back in a few minutes to pay for them both.

He left, and I went ahead and cut the boy's hair. When I finished, I asked the boy to sit in the waiting area. It was a slow day for business, but the boy seemed content to sit quietly and read the magazines, so I didn't bother him. A half-hour passed. Then an hour. Finally, I said to the boy, "Don't worry. Your father will be back soon."

"My father? He isn't my father," the boy protested. "I was playing outside when this stranger came along and asked if I'd like to have my hair cut. I said 'Sure,' so he brought me in here. I never saw him before."

A. Comprehension and Conversation

1. Who is telling this story? How long has he been a barber?
2. Where do you have your hair cut? By whom? How often?
3. Why did Tommy tell this story? Where was he when he told it?
4. What did the man tell the barber when he first entered the shop?

5. What happened when the barber finished cutting the man's hair?
6. What happened when the barber finished cutting the boy's hair?
7. What is a *waiting area?* What kinds of stores have waiting areas?
8. How did the barber find out that the man wasn't coming back?
9. How do you think the barber felt when he heard the boy's story? How would you have felt?
10. How much does it cost to have your hair cut? Would you like to cut people's hair?

B. Vocabulary

Nouns	Verbs	Adjectives
barber	be pleased	content
gas station	come back	reasonable
mechanic	fill up	satisfied
player	go ahead	
service station	protest	
suit	remind	
team	ski	
watch	worry	

C. Expressions

Use each of these expressions in a sentence.
get the oil changed, by all means, it was my turn.

D. Pronunciation Drill

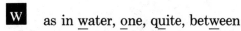 as in <u>w</u>ater, <u>o</u>ne, q<u>u</u>ite, bet<u>w</u>een

work	wise	awake	queen
wide	water	forward	window
warm	went	backward	twenty
wind	word	sandwich	away

unit nine

who's talking?, boy or girl, about who?

Dialogue

ANITA: So this is the Grand Canyon! It's truly spectacular, Norman.

NORMAN: I think it is, too, Anita. I'm glad we came.

ANITA: My brother Peter has been here, and so has my sister Pauline. They both said it was a wonderful sight.

NORMAN: I thought your brother and sister were going to accompany us on this trip.

ANITA: I thought they were coming with us, too. Then, at the last minute, Peter said he had an important business meeting. So he couldn't come, and neither could his wife.

NORMAN: What about Pauline?

ANITA: She couldn't come, either. Her excuse was that she wasn't feeling well. She says she caught a cold from her students at the high school where she teaches.

NORMAN: Don't you believe her?

ANITA: She didn't go on our planned vacation last year, either. It seems that if Peter and his wife don't go on a trip, then neither does she.

NORMAN: My mother and father acted the same way. If one of them wasn't able to go on a trip, then the other wouldn't go, either.

ANITA: You mean that if your mother stayed home, then your father did, too?

NORMAN: That's right. And if he stayed home, so did she.

ANITA: I think that's what's happening with Pauline and Peter. Well, I think we can enjoy the Grand Canyon without them.

NORMAN: So do I.

Answer these questions:
1. What is the Grand Canyon? Where is it?
2. Who is Peter? Why isn't he with Norman and Anita?
3. Who is Pauline? Why isn't she with Norman and Anita?

4. Give an example of something you had to do *at the last minute.*
5. What does *to catch a cold* mean? Have you ever caught a cold from someone? Who was it?
6. What happens if Pauline is going on a trip, but Peter can't go?
7. What happened if one of Norman's parents couldn't go on a trip?
8. If your friends stayed home from school, would you stay home, too?
9. Would you like to see the Grand Canyon? Why? What else would you like to see in that part of the United States?
10. What did Norman and Anita decide at the end of their conversation?

Grammar and Usage

1. Auxiliary Verbs with *too* or *so*

a. Auxiliary verbs with *too* and *so* are often used in affirmative sentences to avoid the repetition of verbs or verb phrases.
　　He speaks well, and she speaks well.
　　He speaks well, and she does, *too.*
　　He speaks well, and *so* does she.
　　He went there, and John went there.
　　He went there, and John did, *too.*
　　He went there, and *so* did John.

b. Note than when *so* is used, the subject follows the auxiliary verb.

2. Auxiliary Verbs with *either* or *neither*

a. *Either* and *neither* are used with auxiliary verbs in negative sentences to avoid repetition of verbs or verb phrases.
　　He doesn't speak well, and she doesn't speak well.
　　He doesn't speak well, and she doesn't *either.*
　　He doesn't speak well, and *neither* does she.

He didn't go there, and John didn't go there.
He didn't go there, and John didn't *either*.
He didn't go there, and *neither* did John.

b. Note that when *neither* is used, the subject follows the auxiliary verb.

Exercises

A. Shorten the following sentences by using a verb phrase with *too*.
   1. He likes the Grand Canyon, and she likes the Grand Canyon. (He likes the Grand Canyon, and she does, too.)
   2. He saw the movie, and I saw the movie.
   3. I am studying English, and she's studying English.
   4. My watch is fast, and your watch is fast.
   5. We go to the beach every weekend, and they go to the beach every weekend.
   6. You took the exam, and your sister took the exam.
   7. Liz left after lunch, and Bob left after lunch.
   8. I have had lunch, and my brother has had lunch.

B. Repeat Exercise A, shortening the sentences by using a verb phrase with *so*.
   1. He likes the Grand Canyon, and she likes the Grand Canyon. (He likes the Grand Canyon, and so does she.)

C. Avoid repetition by shortening the following sentences, using a verb phrase with *neither*.
   1. She doesn't go on trips, and he doesn't go on trips. (She doesn't go on trips, and neither does he.)
   2. Anita didn't go, and I didn't go.
   3. I didn't study, and Norman didn't study.
   4. He won't do it, and she won't do it.
   5. Your watch isn't right, and my watch isn't right.
   6. I haven't read the book, and you haven't read the book.
   7. We won't be there, and they won't be there.
   8. Helen hasn't seen her, and her brother hasn't seen her.

D. Repeat Exercise C, shortening the sentences by using a verb phrase with *either*.

1. She doesn't go on trips, and he doesn't go on trips. (She doesn't go on trips, and he doesn't, either.)

Reading and Conversation: Houdini's Trick

The famous magician Houdini used to tell this story about himself. One day while performing in Louisville, Kentucky, he was showing the audience one of his favorite tricks. In this trick, he made a silver dollar, marked clearly beforehand, pass into the center of an orange without first breaking the skin of the orange. In order to make the trick more complicated, he made the dollar pass into the pocket of a young boy whom he used to choose from the audience. As a matter of fact, he had always arranged beforehand with a boy from the audience who would come up to the stage with a silver dollar, similarly marked, already in his pocket. The audience, of course, did not know this. Everything went well this day until the boy came up on the stage. Houdini asked him to put his hand into the pocket of his coat and take out the dollar. The boy reached into his pocket and instead brought out ninety-five cents in small change. Then he whispered into the magician's ear, "I'm sorry, Mr. Houdini, but I was so thirsty that I just *had* to buy myself a glass of lemonade!"

A. Comprehension and Conversation

1. Who was Houdini? Why was he in Louisville, Kentucky?
2. What is a *magician*? What do magicians do?
3. What trick was Houdini showing the audience?
4. Are silver dollars used today?
5. How did Houdini make the trick more complicated?
6. What did he always arrange beforehand with a boy from the audience?
7. What did the boy take out of his pocket?
8. What did the boy explain to Houdini?

(handwritten top margin: poy 5' / Unit 9 Dialogue / Characters: Anita, Norman)

9. What is *lemonade?* Do you like lemonade? Why did the boy buy himself some lemonade?

10. Do you know any magic tricks? What are they?

B. Vocabulary

(handwritten: New / I. Discuss & Definition 2. Make a sentence with each one)

Nouns		Verbs	Adjectives	Adverbs
audience	stage	accompany	complicated	beforehand
dollar	trick	arrange	famous	instead
excuse		catch a cold	planned	similarly
magician		mark	spectacular	
orange		reach into	thirsty	
pocket		shorten		
silver		whisper		

C. Expressions

Use each of these expressions in a sentence.

so this is _____, at the last minute, small change.

D. Pronunciation Drill

Be careful to pronounce all of the following as words of only *one* syllable.

you're	he's	don't
they're	she's	won't
we're	it's	can't
that's	I'm	there's

The following words have a syllabic *l* sound that makes them sound like two-syllable words.

I'll
she'll
we'll
they'll

New Jersey Generals

unit ten

Dialogue

ROBERT: It looks as though it's going to rain today. Do you think they will play the game in spite of the rain?

JAMES: Yes, I think they will play the game despite the weather. I've seen them play when it was snowing.

ROBERT: I can't believe it!

JAMES: It's true. They did get cold, and they did have a hard time seeing the football, but they played nonetheless.

ROBERT: You North Americans do love your football, don't you? I can't imagine anyone playing cricket during a snowstorm.

JAMES: Of course, there are some sports we don't play in bad weather, but we do play football.

ROBERT: I understand that in some cities you have stadiums which allow people to play despite the temperature.

JAMES: Yes, that's true. In Minneapolis and in Seattle, for example, there are domed stadiums. It's a great benefit for the fans. They can sit indoors in comfort despite the cold or rain outside.

ROBERT: Is the stadium we're going to today one of those domed stadiums?

JAMES: Unfortunately, no. If it starts to rain, we'll have to put up our umbrellas.

ROBERT: You mean we'll sit there in the rain?

JAMES: You did bring your umbrella, didn't you?

ROBERT: Yes, but I hope I don't have to use it.

Answer these questions:
1. Where are Robert and James going today? What are they talking about?
2. What does James say will happen if it rains?
3. Have you ever played any sports in the rain? Have you stopped playing because of the rain? Which sports?

4. What is *football? Cricket?*
5. Where in the United States are Minneapolis and Seattle?
6. What is a *domed stadium?* Why are sports played in such places?
7. What will Robert and James do at the stadium if it starts to rain?
8. Would you watch a game while it was raining? Why/Why not?
9. How does one use an umbrella?
10. Does it rain often in your area? How do people act differently during the rain? What do they do?

Grammar and Usage

1. The Emphatic Form

The auxiliary verbs *do, does,* and *did* normally appear only in negative sentences and questions. We also use them, however, in affirmative sentences to show emphasis or strong feeling.

They don't like to play in the snow, but they *do* become accustomed to it.

I hope it doesn't rain, but I *did* bring my umbrella.

2. *Despite/in spite of; despite the fact that/ in spite of the fact that*

a. *Despite* and *in spite of* are prepositions with the same meaning. Like all prepositions, they are always followed by a noun or noun equivalent.

They play *despite* the bad weather.
They play *in spite of* the bad weather.

b. When the construction of the sentence is such that we must use a clause, these terms must change to *despite the fact that* and *in spite of the fact that.*

We attended *despite the fact that* it was snowing.
We attended *in spite of the fact that* it was snowing.

Exercises

A. Make these sentences more emphatic by changing the italicized verbs.
   1. She *studied* her lesson. I'm certain of it. (She did study her lesson. I'm certain of it.)
   2. He *calls* her every day.
   3. I *wrote* that letter. I am positive of it.
   4. *Call* me again sometime. Please.
   5. I'm sure that she *lives* in California.
   6. Al *took* the book. He told me.
   7. We don't visit them, but we *call* them.
   8. I *did* it yesterday.

B. Fill in the blanks first with *despite,* then with *in spite of.*
   1. He came to class <u>despite</u> his bad headache. He came to class <u>in spite of</u> his bad headache.
   2. I enjoyed myself _____ the fact that it rained.
   3. I like New York in the summer _____ the fact that it is so hot.
   4. _____ the fact that it was difficult, we all managed to finish on time.
   5. Did you spend the summer there _____ the heat?
   6. _____ many problems, I got there on time.
   7. Do you work as hard as your sister, _____ the difference in your ages?
   8. We felt good _____ the fact that we lost the game.

C. Underline the correct form.
   1. Robert insisted (to wait/<u>on waiting</u>) for us.
   2. They have lived here (since/for) many years.
   3. James likes football, and so (I do/do I).
   4. Anita said that she (can/could) not go with us.
   5. I want to find out when (will you be/you will be) back.
   6. I wish I (know/knew) how to swim.
   7. He went (despite/despite the fact that) he was sick.
   8. Did you (say/tell) me that you had enjoyed the trip?

Reading and Conversation: A Wise Judge

There were once two brothers who worked together on their father's farm in South Africa. They were both honest, hard-working men, and they got along together very well. One day their father died. In his will, he directed that the farm and all his property be divided between his two sons.

But the brothers were unable to agree about how the property should be divided. Each one wanted to have the better part for himself. At last they quarreled and, for some weeks afterwards, did not speak to each other.

Finally, they took the case to a judge named S.J.P. Kruger, the same S.J.P. Kruger who was later to become president of the Transvaal. Kruger had a reputation for always being fair. He listened carefully as each of the brothers presented his argument in favor of this or that division.

"The matter is very simple," Kruger finally decided. "We will settle the problem this way: One of you will divide the land into two equal parts the way that he thinks is best, and the other will then take whichever of the two parts he prefers." And that was the way the case was settled.

A. Comprehension and Conversation

1. Where is South Africa? What do you know about this country?
2. Who is this story about? What kind of people were they?
3. What is a *will?* Why do people write wills?
4. Why do people sometimes quarrel over wills?
5. What were the two brothers quarreling about?
6. Who was S.J.P. Kruger? What kind of man was he?
7. What is a *judge?* What do judges do?
8. What was Kruger's decision in this case?
9. Do you think his decision was fair? Why?
10. What do you think the two brothers did after the case was settled?

B. Vocabulary

Nouns		Verbs	Adjectives
benefit	problem	allow	domed
case	property	imagine	equal
comfort	reputation	prefer	fair
cricket	sport	present	hardworking
decision	stadium	quarrel	positive
fan	temperature	settle	rainy
football	weather		simple
headache	will		
judge		*Adverbs*	*Other*
		afterwards	despite
		nonetheless	in spite of
		unfortunately	whichever

C. Expressions

Use each of these expressions in a sentence.
I can't imagine, two equal parts, this or that, in favor of.

D. Pronunciation Drill

ɚ as in h<u>er</u>, w<u>or</u>k, b<u>ir</u>d

early	word	university	perhaps
first	work	were	birthday
third	world	her	verb
property	girl	exercise	turn

© *Laimute E. Druskis*

unit eleven

Vocabulary and Grammar Review

Vocabulary

A. Fill in the blanks with the opposites of the following words.

frequently	seldom	shorten	_____
important	_____	afterwards	_____
war	_____	distant	_____
calm	_____	attractive	_____
indoors	_____	chilly	_____
good	_____	half	_____
health	_____	handsome	_____
fix	_____	similar	_____
complicated	_____	whisper	_____

B. Give the noun form of each of these.

Verbs		Adjectives	
deceive	deception	blind	blindness
demand	_____	important	_____
claim	_____	popular	_____
invite	_____	noisy	_____
joke	_____	excited	_____

C. Fill in the blanks with the correct past and past participle forms of the following verbs.

sell	sold	sold
check	_____	_____
claim	_____	_____
insist	_____	_____
awaken	_____	_____
last	_____	_____
try	_____	_____
turn out	_____	_____
look forward to	_____	_____
feel good	_____	_____
get upset	_____	_____
slam	_____	_____
overcome	_____	_____

spend time	_____	_____
wear out	_____	_____
share	_____	_____
fix	_____	_____
ski	_____	_____
go ahead	_____	_____
mark	_____	_____

D. Supply the correct preposition.
1. We sat in the park for a while.
2. We went _____ Japan on business.
3. She went out and slammed the door _____ her.
4. They insisted _____ waiting for us.
5. It depends _____ whether we go _____ plane or _____ train.
6. She came into the room and smiled _____ me.
7. Did you look _____ the window?
8. The dog jumped _____ the fence.
9. He arrived _____ Hawaii _____ five o'clock.
10. Heat changes ice _____ water.

E. Use each of these idiomatic expressions in a sentence.
that's right, one time, from time to time, at one time or another, in other words, after a while, divided among us, by all means, at the last minute, in favor of.

F. Underline the correct answer.
1. Which of these animals is mainly found in the desert: cow, horse, giraffe, camel?
2. The contraction *we'd* is pronounced to rhyme with which of these words: bed, bad, need, stood?
3. Which of the following is pronounced as a one-syllable word: asked, needed, counted, wanted?
4. Which of the following is pronounced as a two-syllable word: wished, fixed, claimed, granted?
5. Which of the following words is not spelled correctly: quarrel, decision, practize, restaurant?
6. Which are the silent letters in each of these words: knife, talk, Wednesday, listen?
7. People who cannot see well usually use which of the following: outskirts, glasses, airmail, roller skates?

8. Which of the following is a food: arm, sausage, drama, shop?
9. Which of the following words means "say something funny": hurry, trip, sail, joke?
10. Which of the following words means "indoors": even, inside, outside, alongside?

Grammar

A. Underline the correct form.
1. I'm (supposed/<u>supposed to</u>) leave at six o'clock.
2. He doesn't speak English, and his wife doesn't, (too/ either).
3. Did he recommend that she (take/takes) the medicine only once a day?
4. They've lived in Europe (for/since) 1983.
5. You'd better (wait/to wait) until we get back.
6. (I'd/I'll) better wait until next week.
7. I (used to go/am used to go) fishing with my father.
8. You're studying in my class, (don't/aren't) you?
9. She studies in your class, (doesn't/isn't) she?
10. When you arrive, we'll probably (will be/be) swimming

B. Change these sentences to the continuous form.
1. I have lived here since last March. (I have been living here since last March.)
2. Do you watch television?
3. I went to college.
4. She'll come next week sometime.
5. She had worked there.
6. Sharon has studied English for three years.
7. It usually rains on Sundays.
8. Did you talk to James yesterday?
9. They had talked about it when I met them.
10. Will you study in New York next year?

C. Answer these questions in your own words.
1. What is a tag ending, and how is it formed?
2. What is the difference between *I will study* and *I will be studying?*

3. Explain the difference between *I cut my hair* and *I had my hair cut.*
4. What verbs are always followed by the present tense of the subjunctive mood?
5. How is the future perfect tense formed? How is it used?
6. What is the difference between *despite* and *despite the fact that?*
7. Explain why it would be incorrect to say *I used to see him last week.*
8. What are the meanings of the phrases *had better, would rather,* and *a great deal of?*
9. Why is the subjunctive used after *wish, as if,* and *as though?*
10. What is the emphatic form used for?

unit twelve

Dialogue

BARRY: Seeing the sun shine so brightly, I want to go outside. The winter has been long, and I'm ready to walk the streets and visit the parks. Would you like to go?

RITA: Yes, I would. Let's go the The Cloisters. I've heard that the medieval art there is beautiful.

BARRY: I think The Cloisters is located in Fort Tryon Park, isn't it?

RITA: Yes, it's a part of the Metropolitan Museum of Art. There are parts of five cloisters exactly as they existed in Europe in the twelfth and thirteenth centuries. The gardens surrounding the building are beautiful, and the view of the Hudson River and the New Jersey shore is impressive.

BARRY: Wherever you decide is fine with me. Whenever we go to a new place together, I have fun.

RITA: Good. We'll drive up Riverside Drive. It's such a lovely day, perhaps we'll stop along the river and have a picnic. Driving here today, I saw a lot of people already out in the parks.

BARRY: Walking here, I saw the same thing.

RITA: Shall we go?

BARRY: Sure.

Answer these questions:
1. What made Barry decide he wanted to be outside?
2. Where did Rita suggest they go? Why?
3. What is a *cloister?*
4. What is interesting about The Cloisters?
5. Where are The Cloisters?
6. How does Barry respond to Rita's suggestion?
7. What does she suggest they do along the river? Why?
8. How does Barry respond to this additional idea?
9. Where is the Hudson River? What river is closest to your home?
10. Where are the most beautiful gardens in your neighborhood? Describe them.

Grammar and Usage

1. Participles

a. Participles are always used as adjectives and thus modify some noun or pronoun.
> *Seeing* her leave, John began to cry.
> The gardens *surrounding* the buildings are beautiful.

b. Very often participial constructions are used as substitutes for adjective or adverbial clauses.
> When he saw her leave, John began to cry.
> *Seeing* her leave, John began to cry.
> The gardens which surround the buildings are beautiful.
> The gardens *surrounding* the buildings are beautiful.

c. The past participle of many verbs is often used alone as a simple adjective.
> The picture which had been drawn by John was the best of all.
> The picture *drawn* by John was the best of all.

2. *Whichever, whatever, wherever,* etc.

a. We add -*ever* to the words *what, where, when, who,* etc., to form the compounds *whatever, wherever, whenever, whoever,* etc. Examples of the use and meaning of these compounds in sentences follow:
> *Wherever* he goes, everyone seems to like him.
> *Whenever* I go out with John, I have a good time.
> *Whoever* gets there first is supposed to receive a prize.
> Don't pay any attention to *whatever* he says.

Exercises

A. Substitute present participle constructions for the italicized words.
1. *When I arrived* there, I found him sick. (Arriving there, I found him sick.)
2. *While she was coming* from school, Ms. Nash saw the accident.

3. *While she was walking* behind them, Amy saw them enter.
4. The car, *which was traveling* at top speed, couldn't stop.
5. The man *who was playing* the piano was my uncle.
6. The trees *which surround* the park are all in bloom.
7. *While they were playing* in the park, the children saw a bear.
8. The women *who were working* there were all from France.

B. Substitute past participle constructions for the italicized words.
   1. The book *which was written* long ago was his favorite. (The book *written* long ago was his favorite.)
   2. He found the letter, *which was carefully placed* in the desk.
   3. The picture *which had been painted* by Joan Miró was hanging in their living room.
   4. The students *who had been taught* by Ms. Nash spoke the best English.
   5. The soldiers *who were surrounded* by the enemy were easily defeated.
   6. Robert Bruce, *who had been defeated* so many times, had to run away and hide in a cave.
   7. The workers, *who were displeased* with the new contract, began to argue among themselves.
   8. The books *which had been delivered* by mistake were in my office.

C. Fill in the blanks with *whenever, wherever, whatever, whoever, whomever,* or *whichever.*
   1. We saw flowers <u>wherever</u> we went.
   2. He said, "Come again _____ you like."
   3. He also said, "Bring _____ you like."
   4. I will be satisfied with _____ you bring me.
   5. Did the doctor say you could eat _____ you wanted _____ you wanted?
   6. _____ goes there will have trouble with the language.
   7. I'll follow you _____ you go.
   8. You may choose _____ of these gifts you like.

Reading and Conversation: Chewing Gum

The practice of chewing gum has been with us for more than a century. Millions of people all over the world chew billions of pieces (or "sticks") of gum every year.

Chewing gum became popular in the United States mainly because of the work of one man, William Wrigley, who for many years was head of the Wrigley Company. Earlier, Thomas Adams first began to experiment with chewing gum in about the year 1870. It was he who first made gum softer and pleasant to chew. But it was not until Wrigley entered the business in about 1890 that people everywhere began to learn about chewing gum and to use it widely.

Wrigley liked to do things in a big way. In his first year, he borrowed money and spent more than a million dollars on advertising. For years, there was a large Wrigley's advertisement in every streetcar in the United States. People complained that they could not go anywhere without seeing Wrigley's name. Wrigley even sent, free of charge, pieces of gum to every person in the telephone book of every city and town in the United States. Finally, he began to advertise that it was good for the health to chew gum, that it calmed the nerves, and that it helped to keep the teeth clean.

He used to send free gum to every child in the United States on its second birthday. He employed young women who, in loud, orange-striped dresses, would go from city to city in groups of four or five, stand on street corners, and give free samples of chewing gum to every person who passed by. In this way, each woman gave away about five thousand sticks of Wrigley's gum every day. As a result of this continuous advertising, people in the United States naturally began to buy more and more chewing gum.

A. Comprehension and Conversation

1. Do you chew gum? How often? What brand is your favorite?
2. Who was William Wrigley?
3. Who was Thomas Adams?

4. When did gum-chewing become widespread?
5. How much did Wrigley spend in advertising his first year in the chewing gum business? Why did he spend so much?
6. What were some of the ways in which Wrigley advertised?
7. Do you think chewing gum is healthy for people? Why/Why not?
8. Why do you think he had the young women dress in loud, orange-striped dresses?
9. Why is it a good idea to give away a product on street corners?
10. Where have you seen advertisements for chewing gum?

B. Vocabulary

Nouns	*Verbs*	*Adverb*
accident	borrow	brightly
advertisement	employ	
bear (animal)	exist	*Other*
chewing gum	give away	whatever
cloister	pass by	whenever
contract	respond	wherever
enemy	surround	whoever
nerve		whomever
product	*Adjectives*	
stick	additional	
streetcar	continuous	
teeth	impressive	
telephone book	striped	
view	widespread	

C. Expressions

Use each of these expressions in a sentence.

at top speed, it's fine with me, in bloom, (to) use something widely, in a big way, free of charge, as a result.

D. Pronunciation Drill

ʊ   as in b<u>oo</u>k, f<u>u</u>ll, w<u>o</u>man

good	put	cook	pull
took	understood	shook	push
look	woman	stood	should
book	full	foot	could

unit thirteen

Dialogue

JACK: Hi, Nina. This is Jack. How would you like to go to Radio City Music Hall today? I have an aunt who was supposed to go, but now she can't, so she gave me her tickets. My mom also asked me to invite you to dinner after the show.

NINA: I'd love to go, Jack, but I'm supposed to have finished my history assignment already, and I still have hours of work to do on it.

JACK: You seem to be spending a great deal of time on that course.

NINA: I really enjoy it. Up until now, I seem to have been able to finish all my assignments on time, but now I'm falling behind.

JACK: When is the work supposed to be done by?

NINA: It's due today. I ought to have finished it yesterday, but I went to the park instead of working.

JACK: I'll tell you what. Come to the show, and I'll help you do the assignment tomorrow.

NINA: I'd be happy to have you help me. Are you sure you have the time?

JACK: I'm sure. What time shall I pick you up?

NINA: In about an hour. Let me finish this chapter first, then I'll start to get ready. I ought to be ready in an hour. Why don't you help your mother prepare dinner until then?

JACK: Good idea. I'll see you soon.

Answer these questions:
1. Where is this conversation taking place? Between what two people?
2. How did Jack get the tickets for Radio City Music Hall?
3. Why does Nina think she can't go with him?
4. What has Nina been spending a lot of time on?
5. When was she supposed to have finished her assignment? When is it due?
6. What does Jack offer?

7. When does she tell him to pick her up? What time will it be an hour from now?
8. What does she want to do during the hour? Why?
9. What does she suggest that he do during the hour?
10. When is your next assignment supposed to be done? Up until now, have you been able to finish all your assignments on time?

Grammar and Usage

1. Infinitives

a. Infinitives have two forms, a present form and a perfect form. A perfect infinitive is used to indicate a time earlier than that of the main verb of the sentence or clause.
  Present Form: I am glad *to meet* you. (now)
  Perfect Form: I am glad *to have met* you. (an hour ago)

b. Infinitives also have a continuous form. The present continuous infinitive indicates an action which is going on at the time of speaking. The perfect continuous infinitive indicates an action which continues up to the time of the main verb of the clause or sentence. These forms, composed of *to be* and the present participle of the main verb, never change.
  Present Continuous Tense: He seems *to be learning* rapidly. (now)
  Perfect Continuous Tense: He seems *to have been learning* rapidly. (up to the present)

c. The passive form of infinitives is formed with *to be* and the past participle of the main verb.
  Present Passive Form: The work ought *to be done* at once.
  Perfect Passive Form: The work ought *to have been done* yesterday.

2. Infinitives Without *to*

Infinitives without *to* are used after the following verbs: *make, let, help, see, feel, watch.*
  I saw him *leave.*   He made us *wait* an hour.

Exercises

A. Change the infinitives in these sentences from the simple form to the continuous form.
1. Jane seems to study well. (Jane seems to be studying well.)
2. She is supposed to finish it now.
3. He seems to do his best.
4. You appear to enjoy your work.
5. Is she supposed to practice the piano?
6. They don't seem to have any difficulty with English.
7. I ought to do that every day.
8. Do you have to do something every minute?

B. Fill in the blanks with the perfect infinitive of the verbs in parentheses.
1. I was supposed to <u>have left</u> yesterday. (leave)
2. He ought to _____ it last week. (do)
3. They needed to _____ writing the books months ago. (finish)
4. She was sorry not to _____ painting when she had the chance. (study)
5. We were pleased to _____ to the Louvre when we were in Paris. (go)
6. He was thought to _____ unstable all his life. (be)
7. You pretended to _____ out of town, but you stayed at a hotel in town. (go)
8. Tell me what I was supposed to _____. (take)

C. Change the infinitives in these sentences to the passive form, making all other appropriate changes.
1. He is supposed to write the letter today. (The letter is supposed to be written today.)
2. He ought to write it right away.
3. They ought to send the things at once.
4. Was she supposed to deliver it to my home yesterday?
5. She ought to finish it today.
6. Were they supposed to do it last week?
7. You ought to finish the work in an hour.
8. I have to do it immediately.

D. Fill in the blanks with the infinitive form of the verb in parentheses (with *to* or without *to*).
1. They made us <u>wait</u> two hours. (wait)
2. I told him _____ . (leave)
3. No one heard him _____ . (go out)
4. Allow me _____ your work. (see)
5. Did you show them how _____ the game? (play)
6. Did his mother make him _____ the medicine? (take)
7. Don't let her _____ that we're leaving. (know)
8. Can you feel the wind _____ ? (blow)

Reading and Conversation: Sidewalk Superintendents

John D. Rockefeller, Jr., was the man most responsible for the building of Rockefeller Center. Back in the 1930s, when the center was being built, he was walking along the street one day where the construction was going on. He decided to stop and watch the work, but there was a high wooden fence all around the area. Rockefeller found a small crack in the fence, however, and started watching the workers inside. A few minutes later, a guard came along.

"Move along! Move along!" said the guard. "You can't stand there."

"I was just watching the work," said Rockefeller.

"Move along!"

"I am John D. Rockefeller," explained Mr. Rockefeller.

"Right, and I'm the president of the United States," said the guard. "Now move along before I call the police."

Mr. Rockefeller left, but later, in his office, he began to think about this situation. A few days later, he gave an order that small holes were to be cut in the fence at the level of a person's eyes. Anyone who wished to stop for a while and watch the work going on inside could look through these holes. The guards were instructed to give cards to the people who stopped to look. The cards named the watcher as a member of a club of "sidewalk superintendents." Many people stopped and looked, and since that time, the practice of cutting holes in fences around such work has become very popular.

Today, every time a large, new building is put up in the center of a city, there are always holes cut in the fence around it for the use of "sidewalk superintendents."

A. Comprehension and Conversation

1. What is a *sidewalk*? A *superintendent*? A *sidewalk superintendent*?
2. Who was John D. Rockefeller, Jr.?
3. What is Rockefeller Center? Where is it? Where is Radio City Music Hall?
4. Why did Rockefeller stop to look through the crack in the fence?
5. What did the guard say to him?
6. Did the guard believe him when Rockefeller told him who he was? How do you know?
7. What did Rockefeller order to be done to the fences?
8. What do you think is the average height of a person's eyes?
9. Are there holes in the fences around new buildings in your area? Do you ever stop to watch the work?
10. How widespread is the practice of cutting holes in fences around construction areas?

B. Vocabulary

Nouns		*Verbs*	*Adjectives*
assignment	height	blow	average
center	hole	fall behind	responsible
chapter	level	instruct	
construction	member	pick	
course	police	(someone) up	
crack	sidewalk		
fence	superintendent		
guard	tickets		
hall			

C. Expressions

Use each of these expressions in a sentence.
up until now, I'll see you soon, in an hour, since that
time.

D. Pronunciation Drill

O   as in <u>o</u>ld, c<u>oa</u>l, s<u>ew</u>

no	home	own	old
so	don't	know	grow
low	go	row	wrote
slow	roll	told	cold
though	bureau	Joe	known

unit fourteen

Dialogue

FRANK: Welcome to Broadway, Herb. You're a long way from your home in Honolulu.

HERB: That's for sure, Frank, but I've always wanted to see the sights along Broadway—Times Square, the theaters, the shops, and the people. Two weeks ago, I never thought I'd be standing on one of the most famous streets in the world.

FRANK: I'm glad you're here. It's true, Broadway is a famous and interesting street. It's a lot like New York itself. It's a long, changing street which reflects the character of the sections of the city it passes through.

HERB: I had always thought that Broadway was simply the center of the theater district of New York.

FRANK: Many people have the same idea. Broadway passes through Times Square and in this section reflects the character of Times Square with its movie houses, theaters, and stores. But Broadway is a long street which extends north and south far beyond Times Square. At 14th Street, it becomes Union Square just above Greenwich Village. At 34th Street, it becomes Herald Square, a center of big department stores such as Macy's. At 59th Street, it intersects with Eighth Avenue to form Columbus Circle.

HERB: How far does Broadway extend?

FRANK: Broadway is more than twelve miles long. It runs the entire length of Manhattan from the Battery to 262nd Street. Far downtown it is a narrow, crowded street of offices and banks. Uptown, above Central Park, it takes on still a different character. For a distance of seven or eight miles, it is the street which most New Yorkers know—a wide street of apartment houses and small stores of all kinds. Here many of the people of New York live, shop every day, and go to the movies.

Answer these questions:

1. Where does Herb come from? How far is that from New York?
2. What are they discussing? Where does Frank probably live? How do you know?
3. What kind of a street is Broadway?
4. What is the character of the section of New York known as Times Square?
5. What is Herald Square? Where is it?
6. How long is Broadway? What is it like far downtown?
7. What is Broadway like above Central Park?
8. Have you ever seen pictures of Broadway? Describe them.
9. How can a street "reflect the character of the section of the city it passes through"?
10. What is the most interesting street in your town? How long is it? How does it change from one end to the other?

Grammar and Usage

The Position of Adverbs

a. We place adverbs of manner at the end of a sentence.
   Light the fire *carefully*.
   Throw me the ball *quickly*.

b. We place adverbs of time at the beginning or end of a sentence.
   Afterwards, we went to South America.
   They're going to meet us *tomorrow*.

c. We place adverbs of frequency before the main verb and after any auxiliary verb.
   They *always* study with us.
   They have *always* studied with us.
   Don't they *usually* study with you?

Exercises

A. Place the adverb in parentheses in its correct position in each sentence.
   1. He can't visit his parents when they want him to. (always) (He can't always visit his parents when they want him to.)
   2. I read the newspaper every morning. (generally)
   3. Since the baby was asleep, we spoke. (softly)
   4. She saw me in the park. (yesterday)
   5. Do you see him in the park? (often)
   6. They go for a walk in the park on Sunday. (usually)
   7. The class sang the song. (joyfully)
   8. We did our exercises outdoors. (today)
   9. Please fill in the forms. (neatly)
   10. We've been good students. (always)
   11. She's been to Times Square. (never)
   12. Has he been in your class? (always)
   13. I will come to visit you. (next week)
   14. Will you visit me? (often)
   15. I bought my car. (last year)
   16. I water my plants. (every day)

B. Correct the word order in these sentences.
   1. I saw yesterday that movie. (I saw that movie yesterday.)
   2. I went last night to the concert.
   3. He came yesterday to see us.
   4. She gave me this morning your message.
   5. Did you send last week the letter?
   6. Does he come ever to the lesson?
   7. Have you been always a good student?
   8. I've been never to Times Square.

C. Underline the correct form.
   1. I wish you (can/could) go with me.
   2. He (said/told) us where he was going.
   3. She didn't like the song, and neither (did I/I did).
   4. Yesterday I (made/had) my hair cut.
   5. Ms. Nash will not let us (to leave/leave) early.
   6. When we arrived at seven o'clock, they (ate/were eating).

7. If we arrive at seven o'clock, they (are eating/will be eating) their dinner.
8. They suggested that we (waited/wait).

Reading and Conversation: A Clever Escape

A wise judge who served many years ago in a district of Spain was condemned to be imprisoned in a tower because the governor of the district was jealous of his popularity and of the deep affection which the people of the district felt for the judge.

He remained in prison for some time with no hope of escape. One night as he was looking out of the window, he saw his wife standing at the foot of the tower. She was crying sadly.

"Do not cry," the judge called to her, "but listen instead to what I am going to say. Go and bring back a scarab, a little butter, some silk thread, a heavy cord, and a rope. If you do this, you can save me."

The woman left at once and returned quickly with the things the judge had asked for.

The judge said, "Put a little of the butter on the head of the scarab, tie the silk thread around its body, and place it on the wall with its head pointing upwards."

The woman did this. The scarab, thinking that the butter was somewhere above him, began to climb the wall.

The judge waited eagerly above. When at last the scarab was close to him, he picked it up and removed the silk thread from its body. Then his wife tied the cord to the other end of the silk thread. When the judge pulled the cord up, his wife had already tied the rope to one end.

The judge now had only to tie one end of the rope securely within the tower and then slide down the rope in order to reach the ground. There his wife was waiting, happy to see him and surprised that such a simple thing as a scarab had made his escape possible.

A. Comprehension and Conversation

1. Why was the judge condemned to prison?
2. What was his wife doing when he saw her from the window? Why was she doing this?

3. What instructions did he give her?
4. What is a *scarab?* What did she do with the butter and the scarab?
5. Why did the scarab climb upwards? What did the judge do when it reached him?
6. What is thread used for? What is cord used for? What is rope used for?
7. What is a *tower?* Why do you think people build towers?
8. What do you think of the judge's method of escaping from prison?
9. Why are people sent to prison?
10. Of all the items used by the judge and his wife in the escape, which do you think was the most important? Why?

B. Vocabulary

Nouns		Verbs	Adjectives	Adverbs
affection	nightclub	become	clever	eagerly
bank	popularity	climb	crowded	securely
butter	rope	condemn	entire	simply
character	scarab	extend	jealous	upwards
distance	section	intersect	narrow	
district	theater	pass through	silk	*Other*
escape	thread	point	welcome	beyond
governor	tower	reflect	wise	
length		run (extend)		
method		slide		

C. Expressions

Use each of these expressions in a sentence.
that's for sure, far beyond, no hope of escape.

D. Pronunciation Drill

u   as in t<u>oo</u>, sh<u>oe</u>, fr<u>ui</u>t

| room | blue | blew | movie | school | June | rule |
| true | grew | do | who | soon | two | cool |

Hawaii Visitors Bureau Photo

unit fifteen

Dialogue

HERB: Aloha, Frank. Welcome to Hawaii.

FRANK: Thanks, Herb. I'm glad to be here. Thanks for inviting me.

HERB: You must be tired after that long plane ride. Your eyes look droopy.

FRANK: I think it's more than that, Herb. I don't feel well. I must have caught a cold before I left New York.

HERB: I'll bet it was during that snowstorm you had last week. We read all about it here.

FRANK: Yes, that must've been it. Of course, I may have caught the cold from my roommate, Chris.

HERB: I don't remember meeting Chris when I was in New York visiting you.

FRANK: He may have been out of town that week; I forget. He's often out of town.

HERB: Well, let's get you well in a hurry. There are dozens of places which you must see while you're here. After we rest a while, we'll tour the city and the rest of the island of Oahu. Then tomorrow or the next day we'll go to Maui. That's the big island to the east of us. You must have seen it as you flew in.

FRANK: Yes, the pilot pointed it out for us. Herb, all of this sounds wonderful, but first I must get rid of this cold. I won't have any fun as a tourist unless I feel better than this.

Answer these questions:
1. What does *aloha* mean? Where is it used?
2. How does Herb think Frank looks? Why?
3. What does Frank think must have happened before he left New York?
4. From whom might Frank have caught his cold?
5. Where was Chris when Herb was in New York visiting Frank?
6. Where does Herb want to take Frank?

7. What does Frank want to do before he starts touring the islands?
8. Where is Hawaii? What country is it a part of?
9. Name two of the Hawaiian islands. On which island is the capital, Honolulu?
10. What do you do to get rid of a cold?

Grammar and Usage

1. *Must/must have*

a. The verb *must,* which normally expresses obligation, is also used to indicate strong probability.
> John is absent from the lesson. He *must* be sick.
> (i.e., it is strongly probable that he is sick)

b. *Must,* used with this meaning, also has a past tense. It is formed with *have* and the past participle of the main verb.
> John was absent from the lesson. He *must have been* sick.
> They *must have gone* to the movies.

2. *May/may have*

May, used to show possibility, has a past tense form similar to the past tense of *must.* It is formed with *have* and the past participle of the main verb. It indicates a weaker form of possibility or probability than *must have.*
> John was absent from class. He *may have been* sick.
> They *may have gone* to the movies.

Exercises

A. Supply the correct form of *must have* and the verb in parentheses.
1. I must have left my book on the bus. (leave)
2. She doesn't answer the phone; she _____ out. (go)
3. You speak English quite well; you _____ for years. (study)

4. He wasn't at school today; he _____ sick. (be)
5. They _____ home early. (go)
6. It _____ while we were at the ballet. (rain)
7. We _____ at least ten miles along Broadway. (walk)
8. It's dark; someone _____ the light. (put out)

B. Rewrite the following, introducing the *must have* form.
   1. They probably went to the movie. (They must have gone to the movie.)
   2. He probably left his book on the subway.
   3. I probably put it in my pocket without thinking.
   4. He probably forgot to tell me about it.
   5. It probably was an interesting picture.
   6. She probably tied the rope very securely.
   7. They were probably very fond of her.
   8. It probably rained a great deal last night.

C. Supply the correct form of *may have* and the verb in parentheses.
   1. She's not here; she <u>may have gone</u> for a walk. (go)
   2. He _____ her a long time ago. (meet)
   3. You _____ more clever than they thought. (be)
   4. You _____ it on the subway. (leave)
   5. It _____ while we were sleeping. (rain)
   6. He _____ English before he came to this country. (study)
   7. She _____ to bring it. (forget)
   8. He _____ very jealous of her. (be)

D. Rewrite the following, introducing the *may have* form.
   1. It is possible that she saw you on the street. (She may have seen you on the street.)
   2. It is possible that they did it by mistake.
   3. It is possible they knew her for a long time.
   4. It is possible she took it.
   5. It is possible he lost the money.
   6. It is possible I was jealous at one time.
   7. It is possible he was out of town at the time.
   8. It is possible you caught it during the snowstorm.

Reading and Conversation: Word Origins

One of the most interesting of all studies is the study of words and word origins. Since languages evolve from other languages, the words of a language can sometimes be traced to two or three different languages. A word from one language may pass into other languages and develop a new meaning. The word *etiquette*, which is of French origin and originally meant a label or a sign, passed into Spanish and kept its original meaning. So in Spanish the word *etiqueta* today is used to indicate a small tag which a store attaches to a suit, a dress, or a bottle. The word *etiquette* in French, however, gradually developed a different meaning. It later became the custom to write directions on small cards, or *etiquettes,* as to how visitors should dress for and act during an important ceremony at the royal court. Thus, the word *etiquette* began to indicate a system of correct manners for people to follow. With this meaning, the word passed into English.

Consider the word *breakfast. To fast* is to go for some period of time without eating. Thus, in the morning, after many hours during the night without food, one "breaks fast."

Consider the everyday English expression *good-bye.* Many years ago, people would say to each other on parting, "God be with you." As this expression was repeated over and over millions of times, it gradually became shortened to "good-bye."

A. Comprehension and Conversation

1. What does *evolve* mean? How does a language evolve?
2. What may happen when a word passes from one language to another?
3. Do you know from which earlier languages your native language is composed?
4. From what language did the word *etiquette* originally come? What did it mean?
5. What does it mean today in Spanish? In French? In English?
6. What does *to fast* mean? How do we get the word *breakfast* from that verb?
7. What is the origin of the expression *good-bye?*

8. How do expressions get shortened?
9. Give an example of correct manners. Do you always use proper etiquette?
10. See if you can trace the origins of the words for *breakfast* and *good-bye* in your native language.

B. Vocabulary

Nouns	Verbs	Adjectives	Other
bottle	attach	droopy	*aloha*
capital	be composed of	proper	good-bye
ceremony	bet	royal	
dozen	develop	sunny	
etiquette	fast		
island	fly in		
label	get rid of		
manners	indicate		
meaning	pass into		
mistake	point		
origin	(something) out		
sign	put out		
tag	shorten		
visitor	trace		

C. Expressions

Use each of these expressions in a sentence.
on a level with, it's more than that, by mistake, period of time.

D. Pronunciation Drill

∫ as in <u>sh</u>oe, ac<u>ti</u>on, fi<u>sh</u>

she	short	shook	push
shake	shout	fish	wish
shoe	show	finish	wash
shine	shall	position	exception

United Nations

unit sixteen

Dialogue

MANAGER: What seems to be the problem here?

CUSTOMER: I came in to buy a few things for dinner tonight, but when I got to the check-out counter I realized that I had less money than I thought I had.

MANAGER: Well, that's no problem. Why don't you put a few of those cans back?

CUSTOMER: I should have remembered to bring more money. I ought not to have been so careless and forgetful. Now that I'm working full-time and going to school, I have less time to do the food shopping. That's why I'm upset.

MANAGER: You're right. You shouldn't have forgotten the extra money, but we all forget something once in a while. You should've prepared your trip to the store more carefully.

CUSTOMER: I do have a few checks in my wallet. May I pay for the food by check? That way I won't have to go home with less food than my family needs.

MANAGER: As long as your name and address are printed on the check, you shouldn't have any problems, but let me ask my boss, the area supervisor. I'll call him now. In the meantime, you can go back and see if you forgot any items you may need.

Answer these questions:
1. Where is this conversation taking place? Between what two people?
2. What is the problem they are discussing?
3. Have you ever gone out to buy something and then realized that you didn't have enough money? What did you do?
4. Are you ever careless and forgetful? When?
5. What should the customer have remembered? What should the customer have prepared better?

6. Why is the customer upset? Do you ever get upset?
7. How does the customer want to pay for the food? Why?
8. What does the manager think of the idea?
9. When was the last time you forgot something? What was it?
10. What's the difference between working full-time and working part-time?

Grammar and Usage

1. *Should have/ought to have*

a. *Should* and *ought* have a past tense which is formed in the same way as the past tense of *must* and *may*. To the auxiliary verb *have* is added the past participle of the main verb. The form is the same for all persons, singular or plural.

> I *should have prepared* my lessons last night, but I was too tired.
> He *ought to have waited* longer for us instead of leaving so early.
> I *should not have gone* there.
> You *ought not to have said* that.

b. Note in these sentences that *should* and *ought*, in their past tense forms, have a negative significance. They always suggest something which was not done but which somebody *should have done* or something which was done by mistake and which someone *should not have done.*

2. *A few/less*

a. *A few* (and *fewer*) is used with plural nouns which can be counted.

> My aunt bought *a few* books.
> She has *fewer* books than my uncle.

b. *Less* is used with singular abstract nouns and nouns which cannot be counted.

> We have *less* time than I thought.
> I hope you start to use *less* sugar in your coffee.

Exercises

A. Fill in the blanks first with the appropriate form of *should have*, then with the appropriate form of *ought to*. Use the verbs in parentheses.
   1. You <u>should have gone/ought to have gone</u> to see the ships with us yesterday. (go)
   2. I _____ to him last week. (write)
   3. You _____ the correct postage on the package. (put)
   4. I _____ not _____ so careless. (be)
   5. He _____ to bring more money. (remember)
   6. She _____ her trip more carefully. (prepare)
   7. They _____ not _____ that class yesterday. (miss)
   8. We _____ not _____ so much money. (spend)

B. Complete these sentences using your own words. Use the *should have/ought to have* construction.
   1. We went to the movies last night, but we <u>should've stayed home and studied for the exam.</u>
   2. He came home at eight o'clock, but he _____ .
   3. We walked along 10th Street, but we _____ .
   4. You waited for me on the corner of 34th Street, but you _____ .
   5. She did Lesson 10 for homework, but she _____ .
   6. They spoke in Spanish, but they _____ .
   7. I put it on her husband's desk, but I _____ .
   8. You wrote it in pencil, but you _____ .

C. Supply the correct form: *a few/fewer* or *less*.
   1. Do you have <u>a few</u> minutes to talk?
   2. He has written _____ books than his sister.
   3. I smoke _____ cigarettes than I used to.
   4. We drink _____ coffee than tea.
   5. He went to the store with _____ money than he thought.
   6. I've spoken with him only _____ times.
   7. He has only _____ friends.
   8. He has _____ friends than she.

Reading and Conversation: The Fables of Aesop 1

We spoke in the last lesson of the origin of words and expressions. From the fables of Aesop, a Greek writer who lived in the sixth century B.C., have come down many common expressions—not only into English, but into many other languages of the world as well. Each of the stories of Aesop always had a moral, and it is this moral which we often hear expressed in one form or another.

There is a fable of Aesop, for example, about a farmer who was driving his wagon along a country road. Along the way, the wheels of the wagon got stuck in some mud. The farmer got out of the wagon, and, without doing anything about getting the wagon out of the mud, began to pray for help. The Greek god Hercules finally appeared and told the man to get busy and "put his shoulder to the wheel." Thus we often say in English, when speaking of some difficult work to be done, that one must "put one's shoulder to the wheel," meaning that we cannot always depend on others for help. We also say very often, "God helps those who help themselves."

Another fable of Aesop which is popular in many languages is the story of the young farm girl who was going to market carrying a pail of milk on her head. As she walked along, she began to plan what she was going to do with the money she was to get when she sold the milk. She would buy some chickens. The chickens were going to lay eggs. She would sell the eggs and buy a new dress and hat. The young men of the town would fall in love with her. She would marry the richest one, and so forth. Suddenly, with her head high in the air, she struck her foot against a stone and fell. All the milk was spilled, and she had to return home with nothing at all. The moral of this fable is, "Don't count your chickens before they are hatched."

A. Comprehension and Conversation

1. Who was Aesop? How long ago did he live?
2. What is a *fable?*
3. What do we mean when we say that a story has a *moral?*

4. In the first story, what happened to the farmer as he was driving his wagon?
5. What is a *Greek god?* Do you know any other Greek gods besides Hercules?
6. How did Hercules help give us an expression?
7. In the second story, what was the farm girl doing along the road to the market?
8. Why did she fall?
9. What is the moral to this story?
10. What other fables of Aesop do you know?

B. Vocabulary

Nouns		Verbs	Adjectives
boss	pail	appear	careless
can	shoulder	depend on	extra
check	store	fall in love	forgetful
chicken	supervisor	get stuck	check-out
counter	wagon	hatch	Greek
egg	wallet	marry	upset
fable	wheel	pray	
hat		print	*Adverb*
milk		realize	full-time
moral		spill	
mud		strike	

C. Expressions

Use each of these expressions in a sentence.
   once in a while, in the meantime, B.C., a country road, along the way, and so forth.

D. Pronunciation Drill

r   as in right, hurry, store

room	proud	very	car
run	try	direction	purr
red	tree	marry	her
ride	drive	story	fear
Robert	pretty	correct	choir

Pennsylvania Turnpike Commission Photo

unit seventeen

Dialogue

BETTY: Do you like the chicken salad I made?

NANCY: Yes, I do. It tastes spicy and sweet at the same time. It smells good, too.

BETTY: Thanks. I want everything to look perfect. Those friends of mine that I told you about are coming over in a few minutes.

NANCY: How many of them will there be?

BETTY: About six.

NANCY: How long did they have to drive to get here?

BETTY: It's a five-hour drive. I guess they'll be tired. You may know one of them—Carson Yamada. He's an old friend of your sister's.

NANCY: Of course. I remember him. He was a teacher of yours, wasn't he?

BETTY: Yes, he was.

NANCY: How often do you see him?

BETTY: Not often. I'm looking forward to seeing him. How do I look?

NANCY: You have nothing to worry about. You look great. Your food looks delicious. The apartment looks beautiful. Relax and enjoy yourself. Now, tell me again, how soon do you expect them? *(The doorbell rings.)*

BETTY: They're here!

Answer these questions:
1. What are Betty and Nancy talking about?
2. How many people are coming? From how far?
3. What does Nancy say about Betty's chicken salad?
4. Whom is Carson Yamada a friend of? A teacher of?
5. How often does Betty see him?
6. How does Nancy think the apartment looks? The food? Betty?
7. How do people usually feel after a five-hour drive?

8. How did your breakfast taste this morning? How did it smell?
9. How do you feel? How do you look today?
10. Whom are you a friend of?

Grammar and Usage

1. The Possessive with *of*

The possessive with *of* consists of the preposition *of* and a possessive noun or pronoun. The phrase directly follows the noun it modifies.

> He is a close friend *of hers.*
> Yesterday I met an old teacher *of mine.*

2. The Use of *how* in Questions

Note how we use the word *how,* in combination with an adjective or adverb, to ask questions. Some possible combinations of this kind are *how soon, how often, how big, how tall, how late, how well, how much,* and *how many.*

> *How often* does John visit you?
> *How far* is it from New York to Chicago?
> *How soon* do you expect him to return?
> *How tall* is she?

3. The Use of Adjectives after Certain Verbs

An adjective rather than an adverb is used after the verbs *seem, look, appear, feel, smell,* and *taste* when these verbs are similar in meaning and function to the verb *to be;* in these cases, the adjective refers back to and describes the subject.

> The food tastes *good.*
> The food looks *good.*
> The food smells *good.*

Compare these sentences·

> Sara looked *cold.*
> Sam looked at us *coldly.*

Exercises

A. Change the following to the possessive with *of.*
1. She is my friend. (She is a friend of mine.)
2. She is his teacher.
3. Betty has been my student for many years.
4. He is our cousin.
5. They are my family's friends.
6. I could see that it was not his book.
7. We are her mother's dear friends.
8. Isn't he your sister's friend?

B. Change these statements to questions beginning with *how* and the necessary adjective or adverb.
1. They live ten miles from here. (How far do they live from here?)
2. He is six feet tall.
3. The river at that point is ten miles wide.
4. They come here three times a week.
5. He expects them back soon.
6. The book cost you three dollars.
7. She has studied English for four years.
8. She's fifteen years old.

C. Fill in the proper adjective or adverb form.
1. This medicine tastes <u>bitter</u>. (bitter)
2. He tasted the soup _____ . (careful)
3. She appears _____ after being sick. (weak)
4. These apples smell _____ . (bad)
5. They looked at us _____ . (angry)
6. I feel _____ about certain political questions. (strong)
7. I smiled at her _____ . (sweet)
8. You look _____ in that dress. (sweet)

D. Underline the correct form.
1. Do you mind (to wait/<u>waiting</u>) for me?
2. I feel (cold/coldly).
3. He knows her, and (so do I/I do so).
4. We are thinking (to take/of taking) a trip to Nevada.
5. He wants to know where (is she/she is).
6. She is supposed (to do/to have done) that yesterday.

7. I wish I (know/knew) how to play the violin.
8. He gave (to me/me) the book.

Reading and Conversation: The Fables of Aesop 2

In a previous lesson, we read something about the fables of Aesop and of the many everyday expressions in English and other languages which have their origin in these fables.

Sometimes you will hear someone say, "Fine feathers do not make fine birds." This expression comes from the fable of the ugly bird who, coming upon some peacock feathers lying on the ground, put them all together and then tied them to his tail in order to make himself more beautiful. Then he tried to associate with the other peacocks, but the peacocks soon discovered the trick, attacked him, and killed him.

Many times people say, "Looks are deceiving." This saying comes from the story of Aesop about the wolf who covered himself with the skin of a sheep. In this way he was able to enter the farmyard and kill the sheep.

Another well-known story of Aesop is that of the boy who cried wolf.

There was a young farm boy who worked as a shepherd. He had been told that if a wolf came to attack the sheep, he should cry at once in a loud voice, "Wolf! Wolf!" Then other workers on the farm would come at once to help him. One day the boy cried "Wolf!" several times; the men left their work and ran to the boy, but there was no wolf. The boy had simply cried "Wolf!" in order to amuse himself and tease the men. On another day he did the same thing. A third day, the same thing happened. A few days later, however, a wolf actually appeared. This time, when the boy cried "Wolf!" the men thought the boy was only trying to deceive them again. So they continued with their work. The wolf attacked and killed the boy, and also stole several sheep.

A. Comprehension and Conversation

1. What are *peacocks? Wolves? Sheep?*

2. In the first story, why did the ugly bird tie peacock feathers to his tail?
3. What did the other birds do to him?
4. What is the meaning of "fine feathers do not make fine birds"?
5. Where did the expression "Looks are deceiving" come from?
6. In the third story, what is the job of a *shepherd?*
7. Why did the boy cry "Wolf!" when there was no wolf?
8. What happened to him when there really was a wolf?
9. Which of these animals are domestic, and which are wild: wolf, sheep, peacock, chicken, horse?
10. Give the plural form of each of the animals in question 9.

B. Vocabulary

Nouns		*Verbs*	*Adjectives*
bird	tail	amuse oneself	bitter
doorbell	violin	associate with	delicious
farmyard	wolf	attack	domestic
feathers		expect	perfect
ground		tease	political
peacock			previous
salad		*Adverb*	spicy
saying		actually	sweet
sheep			ugly
shepherd			weak
skin			wild

C. Expressions

Use each of these expressions in a sentence.
at the same time, to come upon something, not often.

D. Pronunciation Drill

The ending -*ed,* when added to any regular verb to form the simple past tense, is pronounced as follows:

1. It is pronounced as a separate syllable [ɪd] if the verb ends in *t* or *d*.

    wait   waited (pronounced *wait ed* [wétɪd])
    want   wanted (pronounced *want ed* [wántɪd])

2. It is pronounced [t] if the verb ends in any voiceless sound (except *t*).

    ask   asked (pronounced *asked* [æskt])
    wash   washed (pronounced *washed* [waʃt])

3. It is pronounced [d] if the verb ends in any voiced sound (except *d*).

    play   played (pronounced *played* [pled])
    turn   turned (pronounced *turned* [tɚnd])

unit eighteen

Dialogue

MARIE: I'm really tired. I've had a hard day. I think I'll lie down for a while before dinner.

DONALD: (*He rises from his seat.*) That's O.K. I'll start dinner. Why don't you sit here in this chair and relax while I set the table.

MARIE: No, I'm pretty tired. I think if I lie across my bed for a few minutes, I'll feel better.

DONALD: The bed is busy.

MARIE: What?

DONALD: I laid all of our clothes across the bed, deciding which ones to keep and which to give to the McCarthys. There's no room for you to lie there. Why don't I raise the window and let in some fresh air? That might make you feel better.

MARIE: I thought if I lay still for a while it would help, but perhaps if I just sit still . . .

DONALD: That's a good idea. I've set the mail on the table over there, if you'd like to see it. (*He starts to raise the curtain.*)

MARIE: Please don't do that. I like it dark. It helps me relax.

DONALD: O.K. Take it easy. Dinner will be ready soon. If you fall asleep, I'll wake you when it's ready.

Answer these questions:
1. What does Marie want to do before dinner? Why?
2. What do you do when you are tired during the day? At night?
3. What does Donald suggest she do?
4. Why can't she lie on the bed?
5. What are some different ways to let fresh air into a house?
6. How does Marie decide to rest?
7. Where did Donald set the mail?
8. What happens when Donald starts to raise the curtain? Why?

9. What will Donald do if Marie falls asleep?
10. Who sets the table for dinner in your home? Where do you sit at dinner?

Grammar and Usage

Transitive verbs take direct objects to complete their meanings. *Intransitive verbs* do not take direct objects because the action of the verbs is complete in itself and not carried on to objects. We can test to see if a verb is transitive or intransitive by asking a question with *who* or *what* in the object position. If neither question can be answered, the verb is intransitive.

1. *Raise/rise*

a. *Raise* is transitive; it is followed by a direct object. One always raises something. It is a regular verb.
John *raised* the window. (What did he raise?)
Mary *raised* her hand. (What did she raise?)

b. *Rise* is an intransitive verb and therefore is never followed by an object. The principal parts of *rise* are *rise, rising, rose, risen.*
The sun *rises* at seven o'clock.
Joe *rose* slowly to his feet.

2. *Set/sit*

Set is a transitive verb, like *raise,* and is followed by a direct object. *Sit,* like *rise,* is intransitive.
Mary *set* the book on the table. (What did she set on the table?)
John always *sits* at this desk.

3. *Lay/lie*

a. *Lay,* like *raise,* is a transitive verb. It is always followed by a direct object. One always *lays* something somewhere. The principal parts of *lay* are *lay, laying, laid, laid.*
He *laid* the books on the chair. (What did he lay on the chair?)

They will *lay* the cornerstone tomorrow. (What will they lay tomorrow?)

b. *Lie,* like *rise,* is an intransitive verb and is never followed by a direct object. It is impossible to *lie* something. Instead, something *lies* by itself. The principal parts of *lie* are *lie, lying, lay, lain.*

Your coat *is lying* on the floor.

He *lay* down but could not rest.

Exercises

A. Supply the correct form of *raise* or *rise.*
1. Will you please <u>raise</u> the curtain?
2. The sun _____ every day at six o'clock.
3. He _____ chickens on his farm.
4. They are trying to _____ money to build a new hospital.
5. Martha got angry, _____ to her feet, and left the room.
6. When the teacher asked the question, I _____ my hand.
7. The sun _____ yesterday at exactly 6:20 a.m.
8. Do you think the government will _____ taxes again?

B. Supply the correct form of *sit* or *set.*
1. I always <u>sit</u> at this desk.
2. Yesterday I _____ at a different desk.
3. You can _____ the typewriter on this table.
4. The barber picked up the scissors and _____ them on the counter.
5. You can _____ in this seat near me.
6. Are you _____ down?
7. The sun usually _____ at five o'clock in the afternoon.
8. We have been _____ in these chairs for over an hour.

C. Supply the correct form of *lie* or *lay.*
1. The dog likes to <u>lie</u> in the sun.
2. Yesterday he _____ in the sun all day.
3. _____ on this couch for a few minutes until you feel better.
4. I thought I had _____ it on that table.
5. Your coat is _____ on the chair in the other room.

6. You can _____ your scarf on that desk.
7. The small town _____ at the foot of the mountain.
8. Last night when I was tired, I _____ across my sister's bed and fell asleep.

D. Underline the correct form.
   1. Please help me to (raise/rise) this window.
   2. The sun (rises/raises) in the east.
   3. She (lies/lays) down to rest every afternoon.
   4. You can (sit/set) the lamp on this table.
   5. Have you been (lying/laying) there asleep since two o'clock?
   6. In general, prices are (rising/raising).
   7. Yesterday, farmers (raised/rose) the price of corn.
   8. She (laid/lay) her coat across the back of the chair.

Reading and Conversation: Astrology

People in many parts of the world place a great deal of faith in the stars. Astrology is the study of the positions and configuration of the planets, the sun, the moon, and the stars. The central belief of astrologers is that these positions influence humans and their lives.

The most well-known tool of astrology is the zodiac, a band which divides the sky into 12 equal parts. Each of these parts bears the name of a constellation. These parts are also called signs—the signs of the zodiac. The calendar year, too, is divided into 12 equal parts to correspond with each of the signs. If a person is born between October 23 and November 21, then that person is born "under the sign" of Scorpio. One born between March 21 and April 19 is an Aries, that is, his or her sign is Aries.

The other signs are Taurus, Gemini, Cancer, Leo, Virgo, Libra, Sagittarius, Capricorn, Aquarius, and Pisces. Many people feel that the configuration of the stars when a person is born determines that person's personality. It is not uncommon to hear someone guess another's sign after seeing certain personal characteristics.

Most daily newspapers in the United States have a horoscope column. It is usually a short prediction of possible occurrences during the day and some advice for each of the 12 signs. While many people dismiss astrology as unscientific, horoscopes are among the most popular sections of newspapers, and many people would not think of starting their day without seeing "what the stars have to say."

A. Comprehension and Conversation

1. What is *astrology?*
2. What do astrologers believe?
3. What is the *zodiac?* What are its twelve signs?
4. When is a Scorpio born? An Aries?
5. What is a *horoscope?* Where can one find a horoscope?
6. Why do people consult horoscopes?
7. What is your sign? (Under what sign of the zodiac were you born?)
8. Do you believe that the stars influence our behavior?
9. In what other ways do people try to predict the future?
10. Look at the other people in this room who have the same sign as yours. Are you similar to them? In what ways?

B. Vocabulary

Nouns		Verbs	Adjectives
air	human	consult	daily
astrology	lamp	correspond	dark
band	moon	determine	fresh
belief	mountain	dismiss	intransitive
characteristic	occurrence	influence	possible
constellation	personality	rise	uncommon
corn	prediction		unscientific
couch	sign		
curtain	sky		Adverbs
faith	star		exactly
government	window		pretty
hospital	zodiac		
horoscope			

C. Expressions

Use each of these expressions in a sentence.
a hard day, take it easy, in general, at the foot of, under the sign of, not uncommon, to be divided into, that is.

D. Pronunciation Drill

Practice these -ed endings.

separate syllable [ɪd]	-ed pronounced [t]	-ed pronounced [d]
wanted	dressed	lived
handed	liked	mailed
attended	thanked	believed
affected	decreased	contained
added	jumped	cleaned
accepted	noticed	learned
ended	walked	dialed
needed	stopped	explained
decided	worked	followed
excited	picked	imagined
interested	placed	loved

unit nineteen

Dialogue

MS. NASH: Welcome back to school, class. I hope you all enjoyed the weekend.

CHARLES: I certainly did, Ms. Nash. The baseball team I play for won both games over the weekend —Saturday's and Sunday's. We beat the team from across town both days.

MARTHA: We had some excitement in my neighborhood over the weekend. The supermarket on the corner was robbed of over ten thousand dollars. The thief also stole a hundred pounds of frozen food.

MS. NASH: The thief must have had some help, Martha. A thief could hardly carry all that food and the money, too. It would be too hard for one person to manage all that weight. Janet, why have you changed your seat? You always sat beside Carl. Now you're sitting beside Paul.

JANET: I don't like sitting on that side of the room, and besides that, Paul is helping me with my special difficulties in English. For example, what's the difference between *bring* and *take*? I know several people from the United States, and they seem to use those verbs interchangeably.

MS. NASH: That's right, many people do misuse the words *bring* and *take*. Come here, Janet, and bring your books with you. *(Janet goes to the front of the room.)* Thank you. Now, please take this red pen and give it to Charles in the back of the room.

JANET: Thanks, Ms. Nash. That was a good, practical example.

Answer these questions:
1. Where is this conversation taking place? Who is the teacher?
2. What did Charles do over the weekend?

3. How many games did his team win? Which team did they beat?
4. What was robbed over the weekend? What did the thief steal?
5. If you can hardly hear someone, what would you ask that person to do? Is it hard to hear your teacher when she or he speaks?
6. Whom do you sit beside?
7. Besides English, what other subjects do you study?
8. Did you use to be in a beginner's class in English? Are you used to this more advanced class by now?
9. If I want you to deliver some keys to me, would I ask you to *bring them to me* or to *take them to me?*
10. What does *interchangeably* mean? Can you use the terms *should have* and *ought to have* interchangeably? What about *bring* and *take?*

Grammar and Usage

Special Difficulties

Used to/to be used to

Used to indicates a repeated past action which does not occur at the present time. It is followed by an infinitive. The phrase *to be used to* means "to be accustomed to." It is followed by a noun or gerund, since *to* in this case is a preposition. Note the difference:

He *used to smoke* a pipe.
He *is used to smoking* a pipe and thus does not like cigarettes.
He *is used to* this climate.

Beside/besides
Beside means "alongside of." *Besides* means "in addition to."
He sat *beside* me.
He is taking five courses *besides* English.

Hard/hardly
Hardly is not the adverb form of *hard. Hard* is both an

adjective and an adverb. *Hardly* is an entirely different word meaning *scarcely*.

> He is a *hard* worker.
> He works *hard*.
> He was so tired he could *hardly* walk.

Rob/steal

One always *steals* an object. One *robs* a person or a place of something.

> He *stole* five hundred dollars.
> He *robbed* the bank *of* five hundred dollars.

Bring/take

Bring, like *come*, suggests an action in the direction of the speaker. *Take*, like *go*, suggests an action in a direction away from the speaker.

> When you come back, *bring* a newspaper with you.
> On your way to school tomorrow, *take* this suit to the cleaners.

Win/beat

One *wins* a game. One *beats* an opponent or another team.

> Our team *won* the game.
> We *beat* the other team easily.

Exercises

A. Underline the correct form.

1. I (<u>am used to</u>/used to) sitting in this seat, and I do not want to change.
2. I (am used to/used to) sit here last semester.
3. We (used to/are used to) this climate.
4. Who is sitting (beside/besides) you?
5. Who, (beside/besides) you, went to the game?
6. She (used to/is used to) smoke a lot, but she quit.
7. Five boys (besides/beside) Henry will take the trip.
8. Janet is sitting (besides/beside) Paul.
9. Ms. Nash works (hard/hardly).
10. When he spoke, I could (hard/hardly) hear him.

11. Oh, no! We've been (robbed/stolen)!
12. The thieves (robbed/stole) all our jewels.
13. I'm so tired I can (hard/hardly) stand up.
14. She is a (hard/hardly) worker.
15. They (robbed/stole) the store of ten thousand dollars.
16. Have you ever had anything (robbed/stolen) from your house?
17. Our school easily (won/beat) the game.
18. He (won/beat) the first game, but I (won/beat) the second.
19. She (won/beat) him easily.
20. When you go to the bank, be sure to (take/bring) the bank book with you.
21. She told us to (take/bring) a note from home if we were late for school.
22. As I left for school this morning, my mother said, "When you come home tonight, (take/bring) a newspaper."
23. Has your team been (won/beaten) often this year?
24. Have you (taken/brought) your books from your desk?

Reading and Conversation: Paying the Piper

In earlier lessons we began studying the origin of words and expressions. Occasionally, when speaking of some debt or obligation which must be paid, even at great cost, we say that one has to "pay the piper." A *pipe* in English is a long tube through which water or any other liquid passes. One can also smoke a *pipe* which holds tobacco. In the case of paying the *piper,* however, we are referring to a small *pipe* or flute, a musical instrument.

Consider the story of "The Pied Piper of Hamelin." The story was made popular in English by the famous English writer Robert Browning. It concerns the town of Hamelin, which many centuries ago was visited by a great number of rats. The people of the town tried everything to get rid of the rats, but without success. At last, a strange man dressed in a suit of many colors visited the town and offered to get rid of all the rats—but at a high price. The people gladly agreed. The man then took out a flute or *pipe,* played some strange music, and walked slowly from the town with all the rats following him. A few days later, he returned for his money, but the people no longer wanted to pay him. They complained that he had done very little work and that his price was too high. Again the piper took out his flute and played more strange music. This time all the children followed him out of the town, never to return.

This story was thought for many years to be true. People said it actually happened, but its origin probably goes back to the Children's Crusade in the year 1212, when a boy, Nicholas of Cologne, put himself at the head of twenty thousand young crusaders who left Europe for Jerusalem and who, for the most part, died and never returned.

A. Comprehension and Conversation

1. What do we mean when we say that someone has to "pay the piper"?
2. What is a *pipe?* What other meaning does this word have?
3. What is "The Pied Piper of Hamelin"? Who wrote it? When does the story take place?
4. What are *rats?* What part do they play in the story?
5. Who offered to get rid of the rats? How did he do it?
6. How were the rats and the children of the town similar?
7. Who was Nicholas of Cologne? What did he do? When?
8. Where is Jerusalem? Cologne? Hamelin?
9. Why did the people of the town refuse to pay the piper? How did he react to this?
10. What lesson can we learn from this story?

B. Vocabulary

Nouns

baseball	obligation	supermarket
climate	pipe	thief
crusader	piper	tobacco
debt	pound	tube
difficulties	rat	weekend
flute	semester	weight
liquid		

Verbs	Adjectives	Adverbs
beat	musical	gladly
complain	practical	hardly
concern	special	interchangeably
manage		
misuse		
refer		
win		

C. Expressions

Use each of these expressions in a sentence.
never to return, a few days later, at the head of, for the most part, a suit of many colors.

D. Pronunciation Drill

p   as in p̲ie, hap̲p̲y, hop̲e

pear	people	top
pick	September	hip
pet	apple	pep
palm	purple	nap
part	complete	cap
poor	apartment	soup

unit twenty

Vocabulary and Grammar Review

Vocabulary

A. Fill in the blanks with the opposites of these words.

borrow	_lend_	clever	_____
responsible	_____	narrow	_____
upwards	_____	ugly	_____
to fast	_____	sunny	_____
shorten	_____	good-bye	_____
marry	_____	sweet	_____
wild	_____	fresh	_____
uncommon	_____	dark	_____
win	_____	misuse	_____
put out	_____	careless	_____

B. Give the noun form of these verbs.

appear	_appearance_	direct	_____
marry	_____	pray	_____
dismiss	_____	complain	_____
concern	_____	enter	_____
pronounce	_____	differ	_____

C. Give the adverbial form of these adjectives.

previous	_previously_	accidental	_____
eager	_____	hard	_____
fast	_____	jealous	_____
equal	_____	gradual	_____
interchangeable	_____	expensive	_____

D. Fill in the blanks with the correct past and past participle forms of these verbs.

rise	_rose_	_risen_
lie (recline)	_____	_____
lay	_____	_____
sit	_____	_____
set	_____	_____
raise	_____	_____

pass by	_____	_____
taste	_____	_____
smell	_____	_____
beat	_____	_____
win	_____	_____
put out	_____	_____
indicate	_____	_____
get rid of	_____	_____
climb	_____	_____
blow	_____	_____
borrow	_____	_____
exist	_____	_____
run	_____	_____
reflect	_____	_____

E. Supply the correct preposition.
1. He tried to associate <u>with</u> the new students.
2. Was he very jealous _____ her?
3. Take this _____ the back of the room, and then bring it back _____ me.
4. The wolf covered himself _____ the skin _____ a sheep.
5. Is it similar _____ the one we already have?
6. I get along well _____ all the other students _____ my class.
7. You may borrow that book _____ the library _____ a period _____ two weeks.
8. Some words pass _____ a language from another language.
9. She got angry, rose, and walked _____ the door.
10. You will have to share this _____ the two of you.

F. Underline the correct answer.
1. A person can sit comfortably on a (peacock/ liquid/<u>couch</u>/pipe).
2. Birds are normally covered with (contracts/feathers/ beliefs/hospitals).
3. Which of the following has four wheels: judge, pail, chicken, wagon?
4. Which two of these words rhyme with *rare:* are, bear, fair, far?

5. Which of the following watches sheep: shepherd, curtain, product, nerves?
6. Which of the following do people read by: pipe, tube, rat, lamp?
7. A small opening is a (fence/tower/crack/ticket).
8. Which of the following is a domestic animal: scarab, sheep, rat, wolf?
9. If something is a foot long and we want to make it only half a foot long, we would (lengthen/shorten/widen/instruct) it.
10. Land which is surrounded by water is called an (enemy/egg/animal/island).

G. Use each of these words in a sentence first as a verb, then as a noun.

smell
Verb: I *smelled* the flowers.
Noun: The *smell* of the flowers was strong.

drink	taste	hope	wish
help	heat	joke	swim
walk	talk	ride	bet
sign	attack	pass	design

H. Use each of these idiomatic expressions in a sentence.
at top speed, by mistake, in the meantime, B.C., and so forth, at the same time, in general, for the most part, free of charge.

Grammar

A. Underline the correct answer.
1. I saw him (leave/to leave) the building.
2. He made us (to wait/wait) for over an hour.
3. She is not here; she must have (went/gone) to her office.
4. That woman has (fewer/less) friends than her sister.
5. I have always been a good friend of (Mike/Mike's).
6. Yesterday I met an old teacher of (my/mine).
7. The sun (rises/raises) at about six o'clock.
8. Mary, did you (sit/set) the table?
9. He was caught by the police while (robbing/stealing) a bank.

10. I (used to/am used to) cold weather, so I enjoy visiting Alaska.

B. Answer these questions in your own words.
1. How are participles used? Give some examples of appropriately used present and past participles.
2. Use each of the following infinitives in a sentence: to meet, to have met, to be doing, to have been doing.
3. What are some of the verbs which are followed by an infinitive without *to?*
4. Where are adverbs of time (*yesterday, last week, tomorrow,* etc.) usually placed in sentences?
5. What is the difference between these two sentences: *I used to smoke cigarettes* and *I am used to smoking cigarettes.*
6. Explain the difference between *few* and *less.*
7. Give examples of sentences which show the difference between *sit* and *set.* Between *rise* and *raise.* Between *lie* and *lay.*
8. Where are adverbs of frequency (*usually, frequently, never,* etc.) usually placed in sentences?
9. What do the verbs *may* and *must* indicate? What are their past forms?
10. Adjectives, rather than adverbs, are used after several verbs. Name some of them.

appendix

The Principal Parts of Irregular Verbs Found in Book 3

Present	*Past*	*Past Participle*
beat	beat	beaten
bet	bet	bet
blow	blew	blown
catch cold	caught cold	caught cold
come back	came back	come back
fall behind	fell behind	fallen behind
find out	found out	found out
fly in	flew in	flown in
get rid of	got rid of	gotten rid of
give away	gave away	given away
go ahead	went ahead	gone ahead
lay	laid	laid
lie (recline)	lay	lain
overcome	overcame	overcome
put out	put out	put out
rise	rose	risen
run	ran	run
set	set	set
sit	sat	sat
slide	slid	slid
spend time	spent time	spent time
spill	spilled	spilled
strike	struck	struck
wear out	wore out	worn out
win	won	won

Sample Conjugations

Verb: *to work*

Present Tense

I work	we work
you work	you work
he, she, it works	they work

Past Tense

I worked	we worked
you worked	you worked
he worked	they worked

Future Tense

I will work	we will work
you will work	you will work
he will work	they will work

Present Perfect Tense

I have worked	we have worked
you have worked	you have worked
he has worked	they have worked

Past Perfect Tense

I had worked	we had worked
you had worked	you had worked
he had worked	they had worked

Future Perfect Tense

I will have worked	we will have worked
you will have worked	you will have worked
he will have worked	they will have worked

Present Continuous Tense

I am working	we are working
you are working	you are working
he, she, it is working	they are working

Past Continuous Tense

I was working	we were working
you were working	you were working
he was working	they were working

Future Continuous Tense

I will be working	we will be working
you will be working	you will be working
he will be working	they will be working

Present Perfect Continuous Tense

I have been working	we have been working
you have been working	you have been working
he has been working	they have been working

Past Perfect Continuous Tense

I had been working	we had been working
you had been working	you had been working
he had been working	they had been working

Future Perfect Continuous Tense

I will have been working	we will have been working
you will have been working	you will have been working
he will have been working	they will have been working

Verb: *to see*

PASSIVE VOICE

Present Tense

I am seen	we are seen
you are seen	you are seen
he, she, it is seen	they are seen

Past Tense

I was seen	we were seen
you were seen	you were seen
he was seen	they were seen

Future Tense

I will be seen	we will be seen
you will be seen	you will be seen
he will be seen	they will be seen

Present Perfect Tense

I have been seen	we have been seen
you have been seen	you have been seen
he has been seen	they have been seen

Past Perfect Tense

I had been seen	we had been seen
you had been seen	you had been seen
he had been seen	they had been seen

Future Perfect Tense

I will have been seen	we will have been seen
you will have been seen	you will have been seen
he will have been seen	they will have been seen

Present Continuous Tense

I am being seen	we are being seen
you are being seen	you are being seen
he is being seen	they are being seen

Past Continuous Tense

I was being seen	we were being seen
you were being seen	you were being seen
he was being seen	they were being seen

Present Participle:	seeing
Perfect Participle:	having seen
Present Infinitive:	to see
Perfect Infinitive:	to have seen
Present Infinitive, Passive:	to be seen
Perfect Infinitive, Passive:	to have been seen